NAVAL EDGED WEAPONS

in the Age of Fighting Sail 1775-1865

Cutlass drill. (Author's collection)

NAVAL EDGED WEAPONS

in the Age of Fighting Sail 1775-1865

SARAH C WOLFE

CHATHAM PUBLISHING

LONDON

STACKPOLE BOOKS

PENNSYLVANIA

For my grandfather, Edward B. Furr and my mother Ann F. Wolfe

Naval Edged Weapons

© 2005 by Sarah C Wolfe

First published in Great Britain in 2005 by Chatham Publishing, Park House, 1 Russell Gardens, London NW11 9NN

and

in North America by Stackpole Books, 5067 Ritter Road, Mechanicsburg, PA 17055-6921

Chatham Publishing is an imprint of Lionel Leventhal Ltd

British Library Cataloguing in Publication Data
Wolfe, Sarah C.
    Naval edged weapons in the age of fighting sail, 1775-1865
    1. Great Britain. Royal Navy – Equipment – History
    2. United States. Navy – Equipment – History
    3. Swords – Great Britain – History – 18th century
    4. Swords – Great Britain – History – 19th century
    5. Swords – United States – History – 18th century
    6. Swords – United States – History – 19th century
    I. Title
    623.4'41' 0941' 09033

    ISBN 1861762453

A Library of Congress Catalog Card No. is available on request

ISBN 1 86176 245 3

Designed by Mousemat Design Limited
Printed by Imago in Thailand

Acknowledgments

I would like to thank first and above all my grandfather Edward B. Furr and my mother, Ann Wolfe, whose collection of weapon and research books first interested me in the areas of history and artefacts. I would like to thank Sarah Rittgers of the Smithsonian Institution, Ann Marie Price of the Virginia Historical Society, David Wilson of the U.S. Naval Academy, and the staff of the National Maritime Museum, who graciously allowed me to examine each institution's collection of edged weapons. I would also like to thank the staff at the National Archives, and Robert Gardiner who spent endless hours at the Public Records Office for me. Appreciation also goes to those who assisted me in writing my thesis at East Carolina University: Larry Babits, for directing and guiding my work; Michael A. Palmer, Wayne Lusardi, and Bradley A. Rodgers for reviewing and editing it; and Don Parkerson for his assistance on the quantitative parts. It was from that thesis that this book evolved. Finally, I wish to thank all the researchers who came before me, Harold L. Peterson, P.G.W. Annis, Commander W.E. May, Richard Bezdek, Colonel Robert H. Rankin, William Gilkerson, James C. Tily, Warren Moore, George C. Neumann and Andrew Mowbray.

Contents

Introduction

From the Roman legionary's *gladius* to the Japanese samurai sword, edged weapons have held a unique fascination for people around the world. Many cultures view the sword as a symbol of justice and protection, yet it remains an instrument of violence and carnage. Throughout history, axes, pikes and swords have displayed an enormous variety of form and decoration while retaining a recognisable and underlying structure.

This book will examine how styles of naval edged weapons used by British and American enlisted men and officers changed during the period 1775–1865. It will also demonstrate how edged weapons used by the Royal Navy influenced those used by the United States Navy, and how that relationship eventually changed when the United States developed its own weapon industry. Finally, it will show that weapons from this period evolved in response to social and aesthetic changes and therefore resonate with cultural meanings and symbolic themes.

The study of Anglo-American naval edged weapons is important because it provides valuable information on a topic seldom investigated. Until recently, virtually all studies in the United States focused on topics other than naval weapons.[1] In Britain, researchers concentrated on different periods, but only up to the early nineteenth century.[2] Historians have almost completely ignored those edged weapons used by the Royal Navy in the mid-eighteenth and nineteenth centuries.

Historians need to ask why there is such a gap in the historical record of naval edged weapons. Certainly, the scarcity of examples from this time is one factor. Another is the lack of data. The US Navy Department, for example, kept poor records up to 1800, and most of those that were kept were destroyed when retreating American forces set fire to the Washington Naval Yard in 1814.[3] In Britain after the War Office was established in 1854, massive amounts of documents were destroyed as they took over the responsibilities of the Board of Ordnance. Even so, information does exist in museum collections and surviving primary sources. There are also notable secondary sources including the works of P.G.W. Annis, William Gilkerson, and Harold L. Peterson.[4]

The evolution of edged weapons used by both the British and American navies can be divided into four distinct periods. During the first, 1775–92, both countries relied heavily on foreign weapons, especially on those produced by the German cutlers of Solingen, to supplement their weak domestic industries. Britain had established factories at Birmingham by the beginning of the eighteenth century (an outgrowth of Britain's earlier sword industry centres at Hounslow and Shotley Bridge), but the quality and craftsmanship could not yet compete with the quality and prestige of those produced abroad.

Throughout the mid- to late eighteenth century, both countries lacked any type of distinctive naval axe, pike or even sword. Weapons used at sea tended to be the same ones as used on land. These earlier weapons are important to examine, however, because of their later influence on the design and form eventually adopted for formally regulated naval edged weapons.

From 1793 to 1815 the first weapons developed exclusively for use at sea appeared in both the British and American navies. Axes were modified to meet the needs of the enlisted men, pikes were refined for better use in repelling boarders, and the first regulation officer swords appeared in the Royal Navy. Britain continued its attempts to create a strong domestic industry as their access to the international blade trade was cut off by the war with France. Moreover, during this period government contracts were issued to English cutlers on a scale never again duplicated, helping to bolster the industry. In 1805 the Admiralty issued the first regulation sword for officers and continued to modify the cutlass of the enlisted man as they strove to develop a more efficient weapon. Local cutlers in London and Birmingham often suggested many of these improvements. During no other period in British history were as many presentation swords awarded as those during the Napoleonic Wars. Striking in their design, most of these swords were the work of brilliant artisans.

As in Britain, by the end of the eighteenth century, the US government had established a domestic arms manufacturing system, championed by the Secretary of the Navy Benjamin Stoddert. By 1805 the quality, if not the quantity, of arms produced domestically rivalled that of most European manufacturers.

The end of the Napoleonic Wars in 1815 ushered in a new period for naval edged weapons that lasted until 1840. For the next 25 years, the pattern of officers' swords changed significantly in the Royal Navy as the Admiralty issued a new regulation weapon in 1825 only to replace it two years later in

1827. After 1815, however, cutlass design and production dropped dramatically, causing a depression in the domestic industry that would last for nearly 30 years. Similarly, the unique nature of the presentation swords created in the second period was largely replaced by weapons based on the regulation pattern for the remainder of the century.

In America, sword patterns for officers and enlisted men remained varied in style and form throughout the entire third period as the US Navy lacked any detailed regulations over the type of weapons an officer or enlisted man could carry. The development of axe and pike design remained stagnant during this period as neither navy saw a need to improve upon existing designs.

Between 1841 and 1865, the Admiralty resumed contracts with local cutlers in England and Ireland to supply the navy with edged weapons. Fuelled by the wars with China and later Russia, the navy often made demands that local cutlers were initially unable to meet. However, supplemented by the Royal Small Arms Factory at Enfield Lock and aided by the technological advancements of the Industrial Revolution, cutlers were soon able to provide any quantity that the Admiralty required.

With the exception of the Mameluke hilt carried by flag officers between 1847 and 1856, no new sword patterns were introduced into the Royal Navy during this period for either the officers or the enlisted men, although the Admiralty did continue to improve upon the design and manufacture of regulation patterns as better methods of testing the strength of swords appeared. This period was also a time of increasing professionalism as the means of entrance and training were reformed for all those serving in the Royal Navy.

In 1841 the US Department of the Navy issued the first fully-illustrated regulations regarding officer swords. For the next 23 years, sword development in

America progressed as a new regulation sword was introduced in 1852, the American Civil War erupted in 1861, causing the Confederate states to procure or develop their own naval weapons, and presentation swords developed from being plain or patterned after regulation swords to being unique in design. The cutlass carried by the enlisted men also changed dramatically in the years between 1841 and 1865 as the government altered and refined the design to create the most effective and deadly weapon they could.

After more than 20 years of the same design, the shape of axes carried by both navies changed during the final period. As maritime technology advanced and the possibility of boarding decreased, axes became strictly utilitarian tools used to fight fires and clear battle-damage, and their design began to mirror this shift. Throughout the nineteenth century, the use of pikes continued to decline as newer means of repelling boarders appeared. The design of pikes themselves did not change but the variety carried onboard ships of the Royal and US navies decreased as the three-sided pike replaced the leaf-bladed type carried for over a century.

This study ends at 1865 because the weapons developed by this date did not change again, in either the British or American navies, until the twentieth century. Furthermore, by 1865, artillery and armour on the hull of vessels largely determined the outcome of most naval battles, not edged weapons.

Researching and studying edged weapons

For the past 100 years there has been a debate regarding the use of artefacts as a viable source of historical information. Traditionally, historians disregarded them in favour of documentary evidence. William Hesseltine, for example, argued that an artefact taken out of context and placed in a glass box in a museum could not convey the same meaning it did in the time or place in which people first made and/or used it.[5]

In the 1960s, however, a movement began for the study of material culture and the social life of a group as researched through its artefacts. Lewis Binford argued that a group's material culture could indicate beliefs, actions and values. He felt that artefacts have three functions: technomic, socio-technic and ideo-technic. Technomic function refers to the technological aspect of the artefact, or how a society used technology to adapt to its environment. In the case of naval edged weapons, technomic refers to how people used and adapted edged weapon technology in response to the maritime environment and changing battle tactics at sea. Socio-technic function refers to the use of the artefact in a social manner. An example of this is the use of a sword as part of ceremonial dress or as a symbol of rank. This tradition survives today, as both US and Royal Naval officers carry swords as part of their ceremonial dress uniform. Finally, ideo-technic function refers to an artefact illustrating ideological concepts, such as the use of decorations on a sword to signify nationality, religion, political alliances, and so forth.[6] In 1800 for instance, Napoleon Bonaparte commissioned an opulently decorated dress sword fashioned after the weapons carried by the ancient Romans. This was perhaps Napoleon's wish to force an association between his regime and the great Roman Republic.

Research material and weapon examples for this study come from numerous sources. Since most edged weapons are composite artefacts made of several different materials, they tend not to survive in the harsh oxidising environment of the ocean and are often environmentally filtered from most underwater archaeological sites. Therefore, private and museum collections provide the best opportunity to study naval edged weapons. Significant collections include those at the Smithsonian Institution's Museum of American

History in Washington, D.C.; the United States Naval Academy in Annapolis, Maryland; the Virginia Historical Society, in Richmond, Virginia; the National Maritime Museum in Greenwich, England; the Society of the Cincinnati in Washington, D.C.; and the Jamestown Collection in Jamestown, Virginia.

Although archaeologists seldom recover edged weapons from underwater sites, there are some notable shipwrecks where axes, pikes, and swords have survived in anaerobic environments. These include sword fragments found on British wrecks such as the *Mary Rose*, which sank in the Solent, the stretch of water between the Isle of Wight and the mainland of England on 19 July 1545; the *Sea Venture*, which sank off Bermuda in 1609; and the Duart Point Wreck, thought to be the *Swan*, which sank off the coast of Scotland in 1653.[7] In 1995 Marc-André Bernier and a team of divers recovered smallswords from Sir William Phip's vessels *Elizabeth* and *Mary*, which sank in the St. Lawrence River during the failed British invasion of Quebec in 1690.[8] Since the St. Lawrence is a cold, freshwater environment, the weapons are in remarkably good condition. Lake Ontario has similar conditions, where axes, pikes and cutlasses remain intact on board the 10-gun schooner *Scourge* and the 9-gun *Hamilton*, which both sank in a gale on 8 August 1813.[9]

Besides artefacts, documents provide valuable information regarding edged weapons, including data on numbers produced, manufacturing, inspection techniques and uses. The documents examined for this book include correspondence between manufacturers and inspectors, contracts, reports and recommendations of boards appointed to study specific problems connected with weapons, records of issues, general orders regarding weapons, ordnance manuals, the annual reports by the Chiefs of Ordnance, and catalogues of firms that manufactured or sold edged weapons.

Following the introduction, Chapter 1 provides an overview of the nomenclature and manufacturing history of edged weapons followed by an analysis of those weapons used in Britain and America from the late seventeenth century up to the Revolutionary War. Included is an examination of: the axes and pikes that developed into later boarding weapons; the swords favoured by naval officers during the Revolutionary War; specifically rapiers, broad swords, small swords, hangers and cutlasses. Chapter 2 provides an examination of boarding axes, pikes and cutlasses used by enlisted men between 1793 and 1865. A discussion of the uses of edged weapons in boarding actions is also included as well as an analysis on cultural implications. Officer swords are considered in Chapter 3, since they were often bought privately, unlike the government-provided axes, pikes and cutlasses for the enlisted men. First, the origin and background of the officers corps is examined, followed by the changing size, shape and design of their swords, the regulations regarding them, and their markings. A quantitative analysis of the markings on fighting, dress and presentation swords follows in Chapter 4 along with a discussion of the symbolism behind those markings for the period 1775–1865. Finally, in Chapter 5, the history of manufacturers of edged weapons is examined.

The Evolution of Edged Weapons up to the Revolutionary War

From the dawn of civilisation edged weapons, such as axes, pikes and swords, were instrumental in military conflicts in a time before firearms and artillery decided the outcome of a battle. By the eighteenth century most armies had sidelined edged weapons in favour of firearms, but the navies of the world continued to utilise them in protecting their ships. The eighteenth century was a time of tremendous change in regards to naval history as the Royal Navy expanded and transformed to meet the military needs of the country and America emerged as a nation with its own naval force after the American Revolution. Sailors in both countries commonly used pikes to repel boarders, swords in hand-to-hand combat, and axes to fight fires and clear the deck of debris. These weapons used

by both British and American navies evolved from common axe, pike and sword styles used in earlier centuries, when there was little difference between land and naval weapons.

The Royal Navy of the late eighteenth century was the result of centuries of development, but by 1714 it had emerged as the largest in the world with a fleet of around 250 vessels. As the century progressed, the navy expanded further during a series of wars contesting the European balance of power, in which Britain fought Holland, Spain and France for control of trade and colonial resources, and later the American colonists for their independence. For Britain these were predominantly maritime conflicts, and by mid-century the number of ships in the Royal

STATE OF THE ROYAL NAVY 1775–83

Rate	1775	1783
Ships of the Line		
First Rates (100+ guns)	4	5
Second Rates (84–90 guns)	17	20
Third Rates (64, 70, 74, 80 guns)	99	142
Fourth Rates (50, 54, 56, 60 guns)	23	30
Fifth Rates (32, 36, 44 guns)	42	116
Sixth Rates (24, 28 guns)	44	59
Transports, bomb vessels, cutters, & other small vessels	38	85
Total	**267**	**457**

Navy had increased, by one reckoning, to 432, and by 1783 to a total of 617.

The supply and administration of this growing force was the responsibility of the Navy Board, established in 1546 by Henry VIII. Headed by the Comptroller (a senior naval officer), it was specifically charged with the design, construction and refitting of the navy's ships, the running of the Royal Dockyards – the biggest industrial enterprises of their day – and the procurement or manufacture of all the navy's stores, equipment and victuals. Although it was a permanent bureaucracy, the Navy Board was subordinate to the Admiralty, a politically appointed body whose composition altered with each change of government. The Admiralty dictated policy and directed the navy's strategy in wartime, and although it usually included senior naval officers, its head, the First Lord, was more often than not a civilian politician. Dating from 1628, this had begun as the post of Lord High Admiral, but the power and responsibility was then shared among the 'Lords Commissioners for Executing the Office of Lord High Admiral', commonly called the Admiralty Board. Curiously, neither board controlled the supply of the navy's great guns, which were the responsibility of an entirely independent Ordnance Board that also supplied the army's artillery.

As the navy increased in size, the Admiralty faced a difficult problem of manning the fleet in wartime when, it has been estimated, the combined requirements of merchant marine and naval mobilisation far exceeded the total number of professional seamen available. Higher wages, less discipline and the prospect of leave between voyages made the merchant service a more attractive option to most sailors. Consequently, the Admiralty relied more and more on impressments. The Press Gang largely confined its activity to those who followed a sea trade, but later, as the need for men increased, various

quota schemes pulled in many more landsmen and those unfitted for a life at sea. In peacetime the navy could usually rely on volunteers, where, apart from the romantic call of the sea, a naval career offered freedom from the hunger and uncertainty that was the lot of many agricultural and industrial workers in the eighteenth century. The navy, therefore, had become used to training men while actually at sea, and this extended beyond seamanship to handling both great guns and small arms, including drills with edged weapons – cutlasses and boarding pikes.

Most officers came from the professional classes and country gentry, some from families with a long tradition of naval service. There were some younger sons of the aristocracy, who because of primogeniture were forced to earn their own living rather then inherit it, but for all there was little formal training ashore that was regarded as valuable. Most entered as a 'captain's servant' and learned seamanship, navigation and naval fighting skills as they went along. However, they generally came from backgrounds where the use of firearms and swords was inculcated from an early age.

The Peace of Paris in 1763 formally ended the Seven Years War and ensured British dominance over other continental powers in North America. Peace was short-lived, however, and the country soon entered into a war with their American colonies. Aggravated by the lack of representation in Parliament and determined to achieve independence, the colonies formed the Continental Army to challenge Britain's large, organised military force. The Revolutionary War, which lasted from 1775 to 1783 ended two centuries of British rule for most of the North American colonies and created the modern United States of America.

In October 1775 the US Congress started planning for aggressive action against Britain by establishing the Continental Navy to intercept British

NUMBER OF SAILORS AND OFFICERS IN THE ROYAL NAVY 1775–83

Rate	Number
Flag Officers	
Admirals	41
Vice-Admirals	42
Rear-Admirals	49
Post Captains	495
Commanders	319
Lieutenants	2003
Seamen	110,000
Total	**112,949**

transport and supply ships. In the following months, they authorised the construction of two sloops of war, 13 frigates, and three 4-gun ships. Although the government ordered larger vessels, smaller vessels such as schooners, sloops and brigs constituted the majority of the Continental Navy. Most captains favoured schooners over other vessel types since they sailed closer to the wind than square-rigged ships, were quick to manoeuvre, and required a smaller crew, as there were fewer sails to work. The use of schooners as warships gave the Continental Navy a distinct advantage over the larger British warships. Along with the Continental Navy, General George Washington's fleet of schooners, state navies and

STATE OF THE CONTINENTAL NAVY, 1 JANUARY 1779

Rate (guns)	Number in the Continental Navy*
Ship-of-the-line (74)	1
Frigates (24, 32, 36, 40, 44)	19
Ship-Rigged Vessels (10, 18, 20, 24, 42)	12
Cutters (10, 14, 18)	3
Gondola (3)	8
Galley (6, 8)	6
Lugger (10)	1
Brigs/Brigantines (10, 12, 14, 16)	10
Sloops (4, 10, 12)	12
Schooners (8)	14
Xebecs (8)	2
Packets	9
Total	**97**

Numbers include those in George Washington's Fleet, on Lake Champlain, and the Mississippi River.

PRIVATELY ARMED VESSELS TO WHICH LETTERS OF MARQUE WERE ISSUED BY THE CONTINENTAL CONGRESS

Rate	Number
Ships	301
Brigs and brigantines	541
Schooners and sloops	751
Boats and galleys	104
Total	**1697**

privateers assisted in capturing merchant ships and in providing supplies to the Continental Army.

Initially, Congress established a Naval Committee, later renamed the Marine Committee, to handle the affairs of its small navy. In 1779, however, the size of the navy grew to the point where Congress needed a larger and more complex organisation, so it created the Board of Admiralty. A Secretary of the Marine headed the office, supported by members of Congress and three paid commissioners. In 1781, the department was reorganised with General Alexander McDougal as the secretary, and Robert Morris as the Agent of Marine. This system was loosely based on that used by the Royal Navy for centuries.

In December 1774, Congress appointed Esek Hopkins the commander-in-chief of the navy. Hopkins' captains were Abraham Whipple, Nicholas Biddle, J.B. Hopkins and John Hazard, men mainly from Rhode Island. In February 1776, Hopkins set sail on his first cruise to guard the eastern coast of North America. After disobeying orders and extending his cruise down to the Bahamas Islands to capture British stores at Nassau, New Providence, the Navy Department dismissed him from his office. His lieutenant, John Paul Jones, was given command of Hopkins' flagship *Alfred*, and subsequently no naval commander-in-chief was appointed.

Battles at sea were complicated and challenging events, fought in the same general manner for centuries. In 1775, the Continental Congress issued orders for how captains should prepare for battle:

NUMBER OF SAILORS AND OFFICERS FIGHTING FOR THE CONTINENTAL NAVY 1776–83

Rank	Number
Captains/Commodores	57
Lieutenants	142
Marine Corps (Captains/Lieutenants)	120
Seamen	58,000*
Total	**58,319**

About 55,000 American sailors served aboard privateers, capturing British ships in the Atlantic, the Caribbean, and even between Ireland and England.

When in sight of the ship or ships of the enemy, and at such other times as may appear to make it necessary to prepare for engagement, the Captain shall order all things in his ship in a proper posture for fight, and shall in his own person, and according to his duty, heart on [to act courageously] and encourage the inferior officers and men to fight courageously, and not to behave themselves faintly or cry quarters on pain of such punishment as the offence shall appear to deserve for his neglect.[1]

After preparing the ship for battle, each man would receive an axe, pike or cutlass.

Axes

The term 'axe' first appears in naval documents in the seventeenth century,[2] and by the 1790s, appeared in ship manifests, armoury receipts, and ordnance lists as battle-axes, axes, or hatchets.[3] Sailors mainly used axes to clear the deck of fallen and tangled rigging and to prevent the spread of fire. From the earliest times, fire was one of the deadliest hazards a vessel's crew faced. If a ship came under fire from a shore battery, for example, there was the danger of a red-hot shot becoming lodged in its timbers or masts and setting the vessel ablaze. The only way to fight these hazards was to use an axe to cut away the surrounding wood, then use the pointed head to pry the shot loose. They also used the slanting shape of the blade to clear decks of lines and broken timbers, and to drag debris across the decks and pitch it over the side. The axe's value as a fire-fighting tool ensured its place on board a wooden warship for centuries.

Axes consist of two specific pieces: the head and the handle. Each part of the head has a specific name identified by holding the handle in the right hand and the metal head in the left. The cutting edge is the blade. The side of the head facing up is the face. The bottom of the blade is the heel, while the top consists of the leading edge. Opposite the blade is the poll. The handle fits into the axehead through the eye, and the other end of the handle is the butt.

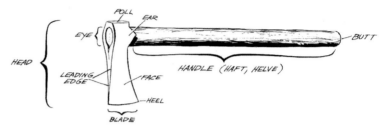

Axe nomenclature. (Courtesy of George C. Neumann, *Swords & Blades of the American Revolution*)

In the seventeenth and eighteenth centuries in both England and America, axes were hand-forged by individual smiths. A blacksmith started an axe by heating a piece of iron until it would bend around a circular piece of metal called a mandrill. This created the eye of the axe. Secondly, he inserted a piece of hard steel between the folded edges to create the cutting edge or blade. Hard steel was used for this part since it could withstand the heavy blows used when cutting wood. Thirdly, he welded the blade to the rest of the axe by forging and hammering it and, in later models, welded a spike head to the poll. Finally, he finished the blade by tempering and polishing the head.

Most axes used in the earlier years of the English colonies came from Europe with the French, Spanish and English settlers. During the seventeenth century, English merchants brought axes with them to trade with the Indian tribes. These early trade axes became the model for later boarding axes used by both the Royal and American navies. The colonists also produce some axes domestically after 1620, as evidenced by archaeological excavations at Jamestown, Virginia. In the 1950s, archaeologists discovered a forge where axe, sword and tool production took place.[4] A researcher can distinguish early American axes from those manufactured in Europe by their cruder construction. Although skilled, blacksmiths had to contend with an undeveloped industry, and a lack of proper tools and facilities.

During the seventeenth and eighteenth centuries, three different types of axes were imported or made domestically in America. The first type was the round poll axe, which had widespread popularity.[5] The axehead averaged 7in (17.8cm) in length, 3in (7.6cm) in width, and around 2lbs (0.9kg) in weight. Over the course of the century, axe width and thickness changed. By 1700, length varied between 3 to 6in (7.6 to 15.2cm), but width remained around 2in (5cm). These changes occurred as colonial blacksmiths developed an axe distinctive to American needs (clearing land, building homes and so forth).[6] The second type of axe was the square poll, which gained widespread popularity around 1700, and remained popular with both the American and Royal navies through 1815.[7] It was a typical European pattern with a flattened face and an indention on the rear part of the axe head. The average length was

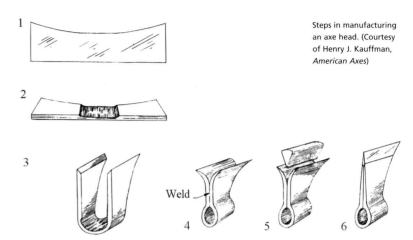

Steps in manufacturing an axe head. (Courtesy of Henry J. Kauffman, *American Axes*)

between 3 to 5in (7.6 to 12.7cm), and anywhere from 1 to 3in (2.5 to 7.6cm) in width.

Of all the different types of axes used on the Continent and in America, the spiked axe had the greatest influence on boarding axes later used by the British and American navies. Modified from the halberd-headed tomahawk carried in the seventeenth century, the head was rounded with downward curving ends. It averaged between 5 and 8in (12.7 to 20.3cm) in length, and between 1 and 2in (2.5 to 5cm) in width. The poll terminated in a downward-curving flat spike almost equal in length to the head with lobe-shaped langets that secured the head to an ash staff. The main difference between the two weapons was that the spike staff found on halberds was not preserved on boarding axes. By the late eighteenth century, the Continental Navy had adopted the spiked axe for use onboard their ships. Since axes were utilitarian objects, the Ordnance Board found little reason to change the design or shape until after the 1790s.

Basic axe profiles. (Courtesy of George C. Neumann, *Swords & Blades of the American Revolution*)

Colonial axes recovered from Jamestown, Virginia. (National Park Service)

Pikes

Although firearms began to dominate the battlefield from the fourteenth century, polearms did not disappear immediately. The first firearms were inaccurate and slow to reload, so most militaries relied on polearms such as pikes to protect musketeers and allow them enough time to reload. As technology advanced, armies in Europe replaced pikes with the bayonet, effectively merging the polearm and the firearm.[8] During the Revolutionary War, however, the American colonies suffered a shortage of firearms and some troops had to depend on pikes.[9]

The first polearms introduced into America came with Spanish explorers in the sixteenth century. A century later, the English introduced the halberd (a combination axe head and pike mounted on a long handle) and spontoon (a short pike with a leaf-shaped head). Archaeologists have recovered a ceremonial halberd and ten four-sided, diamond-shaped pikes from the cellar of James Fort dating to *circa* 1610.[10] English sergeants mainly carried halberds as a sign of rank and to signal commands to their companies.

Although the halberd dated to the fourteenth century, the English had no set rules for its decoration and design. The main parts consist of the pike head balanced by a fluke and sharp point, averaging 6 to 8ft (1.8 to 2.4m) in length. Some historians believe that the first English naval axe was a type of spiked tomahawk with a spearhead similar in design to a halberd.[11]

Like the halberd, the spontoon has three main parts: the head, base and spear point. The head comprises the entire metal portion, averaging between 8 to 15in (20.3 to 38cm) in length, and the portion of the pike connecting to the staff is the base, averaging 12 to 16in (30.4 to 40.6cm). The strongest part of the pike is the spear point, which makes up the cutting edge. The colonial spontoon later developed into the leaf-headed pike used by the Royal and American navies.

Unfortunately, unlike axes, few written documents have survived that deal with the manufacture of boarding pikes. What researchers do know is that, like axes, pikes were hand-forged in both America and England until the mid-nineteenth century, after which they were cast in moulds. Furthermore, since boarding pikes were uncomplicated weapons, a smith could manufacture them from one piece of metal.

Swords

The final edged weapon used at sea was the sword, which, like the axe and pike, evolved from land models. Swords are made of two main parts: the blade and the hilt. Each side of the blade has a specific name identified by standing with the sword hilt in the left hand and the blade in the right. The side of the blade facing up is the obverse; the opposite is the reverse. Blades can be either double-edged or single, and come in curved and straight variants. The blade consists of three parts: the tang, forte and foible. The forte is the strongest part of the blade, whereas the foible is the weakest. The front is the cutting edge; the back, usually the dull edge, is called the spine. The fuller is a shallow groove that runs the length of the blade on both sides. Contrary to popular belief, the fuller was not a blood gutter, but rather

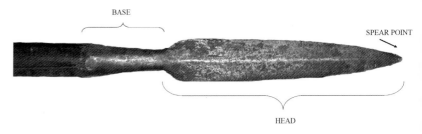

BASE

SPEAR POINT

HEAD

Pike nomenclature. (Author)

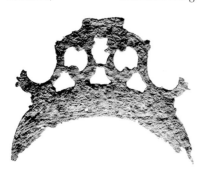

Ceremonial halberd recovered from James Fort, Virginia. (National Park Service)

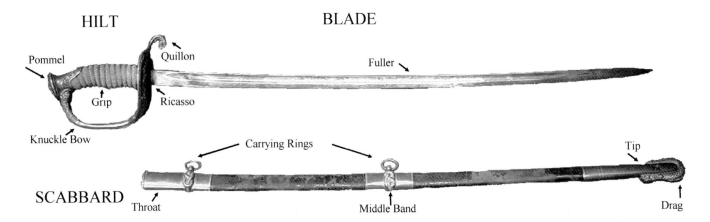

HILT   BLADE

Pommel   Quillon   Fuller

Grip   Ricasso

Knuckle Bow

Carrying Rings   Tip

SCABBARD   Drag
        Throat   Middle Band

Sword nomenclature.
(Author)

a way to lighten the blade without weakening it. The main parts of the hilt are the grip, pommel, knuckle bow and guard. The tang fits through the grip and pommel to secure the blade to the hilt.

Today historians debate over the origin of the word sword. It is, however, cognate with the Anglo-Saxon word *sweord* or *suerd*, Scandinavian *svaird*, Danish *svaerd*, old German *svert*, and Old English and Scottish *swerd*.[12] In past years, sword collectors use the term sword as a generic word to describe numerous variants, including such ancient weapons as the *epis*, *gladius*, and *spatha*. Medieval swords such as the hand-and-a-half (or bastard), claymore, broadsword, rapier and small sword are further variations. Modern weapons include the hanger, cutlass, sabre, backsword and falchion, all designed for cutting, thrusting, or both.

A single artisan did not complete a sword by himself; a forger, grinder, polisher and decorator all worked together to produce a single item. In the first step, the forger prepared the blade. During the seventeenth and eighteenth centuries, manufacturers produced swords by the traditional method of quenching and tempering as quenching produced harder yet more flexible blades than previously examples.

Blades were first forged from a square bar commonly called a skelp. To make the skelp, blacksmiths heated the iron ore to a temperature between 900^0 and 2012^0 Fahrenheit (482^0 and 1100^0 Celsius).[13] They achieved a higher furnace temperature by heating charcoal with air, blown into the furnace either by a natural draught or by bellows. Sometimes inadequate heating of the iron ore occurred, so little absorption of carbon with the formation of iron carbide took place. The blacksmith would then reheat the metal until it reached a red-hot colour, and hammer out as much of the slag as possible. Then he pounded the blade until it was longer than the desired length and shaped and formed the fullers. Sometimes the blade bent and needed to be corrected by hammering it straight on an anvil. In the next step, he formed the tang from wrought iron and welded it to the blade.[14]

After forging, the blade was soft and flexible, so it needed to be tempered to increase its hardness and elasticity. In this step, a skilled worker who had the eye to detect the temperature best suited to the steel determined the blade quality. He held the blade in the heat of a charcoal furnace to harden it. Once the blade was red, he removed it and placed it

An eighteenth-century view of a Parisian cutler shop where workers forged, fabricated and sold blades. (Dover Pictorial Archives Series)

in cold salt-water, resulting in a hard, brittle, and slightly warped blade. It was then heated again, this time until it was blue, not red, and then cooled rapidly in water. Only then would the blade have the appropriate hardness and elasticity.[15]

After tempering, the grinder fashioned the blade into the proper size by using a coarse grindstone on the entire blade excluding the point. He then ran a second, finer grindstone over the entire blade. Sometimes during the process the blade bent, but could be repaired by heating the blade to a blue heat, quickly straightening it, and then cooling it with water.

After forging and tempering, the polisher used emery or corundum on a buff-wheel to remove marks produced by the grindstone, and create a smooth finish on the blade. The blade would be straightened again, followed by a second, lighter polishing.

During the final stage of manufacturing, a smith etched ornamental symbols on the blade. He first coated the blade with a varnish or wax that resisted the effects of nitric acid. Once dried, the design was carved out of the wax, leaving those areas exposed. He then coated the blade in acid that attacked the uncovered parts of the blade, leaving them in an oxidised state. He then removed the varnish with turpentine and cleaned the blade with alcohol.[16]

After the blade was finished, a different smith would create the hilt. In England it was common for London smiths to order the blade from the smiths of Solingen, Germany and the hilt from a local manufacturer before assembling the item for sale. The method used for hilt production differed considerably from that of the blade. In the first step, the smith produced the body or foundation, which was made of wood, then covered it in strips of copper,

Polishing shop where workers embossed, gilded and embellished guards and hilts before assembling swords. (Dover Pictorial Archives Series)

gold, or silver. Since these metals are softer than iron, minimal heat was required to shape them. If decorated, the smith attached mouldings in a similar metal to the rest of the hilt.[17] Before 1800, an experienced smith or jeweller manufactured one hilt at a time. With the advent of the Industrial Revolution, after 1800 hilts were increasingly mass-produced using a mould.

In the final step of sword production, a smith produced the scabbard and sword belt, which protected the blade when not in use. Most land-service swords had steel scabbards, but these would rust easily in a salt-water environment, so naval weapons had leather ones. The smith measured the blade, cut and sewed two separate pieces of leather together, and secured them with two metal bands to hold the leather together. Carrying rings were attached to the bands so the sword could be hung from a belt. Finally, a drag covered and protected the tip of the blade.[18]

Of all the different sword types used at sea, five variants dominated during the eighteenth century: rapiers, broadswords or basket-hilt swords, small swords, hangers and cutlasses. These styles were popular in the Royal Navy throughout the century, and influenced the weapons carried by officers of the Continental Navy during the 1770s and 1780s. Archaeologists have recovered numerous examples of each variant from shipwrecks in America and Europe.

Throughout the Middle Ages, knights used double-edged swords, axes and lances. By the fifteenth and sixteenth centuries, however, changing military

ENGLISH SHIPWRECKS WITH RECOVERED EDGED WEAPONS

Vessel/Site Location	Year Lost	Location	Artefacts
Mary Rose	1545	Solent, UK	Pikes & sword hilts
Alderney Wreck	1592	Channel Isles	Sword hilt
Jamestown	1607	Virginia	Rapier hilt
Sea Venture	1609	Bermuda	Basket sword hilt
Duart Point Wreck	1653	UK	Rapier hilt
Phip's Fleet	1690	Quebec	Smallsword hilt
Port Royal Site	1692	Jamaica	Sword hilt
Henrietta Marie	1701	Florida	Hangers (2)
HMS *Stirling Castle*	1703	Kent, UK	Hanger and smallsword
HMS *Hazardous*	1706	UK	Smallsword or rapier
HMS *Feversham*	1711	Nova Scotia	Sword hilts
HMS *Dragon*	1712	Alderney	Sword
HMS *Maidstone*	1747	Noirmoutier	Hanger hilt
HMS *Fowey*	1748	Florida	Cutlass, boarding axe
Boscawen	1759	Lake Champlain	Pike
HMS *Charon*	1778	Virginia	Scabbard
Yorktown Wreck	1781	Virginia	Rapier
HM Brig *DeBraak*	1798	Delaware	Smallsword and rapiers
Pacific Reef Wreck	1800s	Florida Keys	Cutlass blades

tactics, the availability of new materials and advances in technology greatly affected the form and function of most edged weapons.[19] The main influence was the increased use of projectile weapons such as crossbows and muskets. As projectile weapons developed, the need for full body armour decreased, allowing troops greater mobility. This affected military tactics as leaders began to rely on foot over mounted units.[20]

Soldiers had less body protection but could move more freely, so they needed a weapon to reflect these changes. Swords needed to be lighter, with thrusting blades, and the user more skilled then in previous times. The answer was the rapier, which replaced the larger and heavier broadswords and claymores of the Middle Ages. The nobility in particular liked rapiers when settling disputes by personal combat.[21]

The origin of the word rapier is uncertain, but it may derive from the Spanish word *espada ropera* or 'robe sword'.[22] The rapier was a light weapon with a straight, double-edged, pointed blade. As fencing developed in the sixteenth and seventeenth centuries, rapiers progressively became longer, narrower and lighter until suitable only for thrusting. The blade length grew so long that British Parliament passed an edict limiting the rapier to no more than 3ft because it was difficult to wield, as well as being a public nuisance.[23]

Rapiers first appeared in England in 1560.[24] By the seventeenth century, they became the preferred

Rapier excavated at Jamestown, Virginia. (National Park Service)

Rapier grip recovered from the wreck of the *Swan*. (National Park Service)

dress swords, and archaeologists have recovered examples from such colonial shipwrecks as the *Swan*, which sank in 1653, HMS *Hazardous*, which sank in 1706, and the brig HM Brig *DeBraak*, which sank in 1798.

During the mid-sixtenth century the use of broadswords at sea rose in popularity. In the 1980s, archaeologists recovered the earliest recorded sample used by the Royal Navy from the Tudor warship *Mary Rose*, which sank off the south coast of England in 1545.[26] The recovered sword has a heavy blade and a guard that completely enclosed the user's hand with a system of wide connecting bars, providing an effective guard against cutting strokes.

Another popular broadsword style was the Scottish basket hilt. Excavations at Jamestown, Virginia, and from shipwreck sites such as the *Sea Venture*, a 300-ton English vessel that sank off Bermuda in 1609, have produced numerous examples.[27] Although associated with Scotland today, the broadsword actually originated in Italy. Instead of plain interconnecting bars, such as those recovered from the *Mary Rose*, the owner could order a basket hilt decorated with circles and hearts if he could afford the additional work.

weapon in Britain and its colonies in America, and numerous specimens have been recovered from Virginia and New England. Officers wore rapiers as signs of social status, rank, and in accordance with contemporary tastes and fashions. They were differentiated by the materials (gold or iron) and decorations (ornate or plain) used on the hilt, the quality of the blade, and by the swordsmith who produced it.[25] For a brief time, officers preferred rapiers for their

Basket hilt from a broadsword recovered from the wreck of the *Sea Venture*. (Courtesy of Academic Press, '*Sea Venture* Second interim report – part 2: the artifacts', in *International Journal of Nautical Archaeology and Underwater Exploration* by Allan J. Wingwood)

Rapier hilts recovered from the wreck of HM Brig *DeBraak*. (Delaware State Museums)

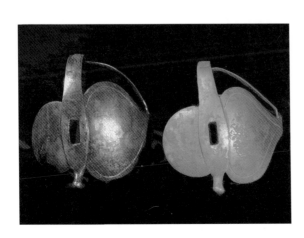

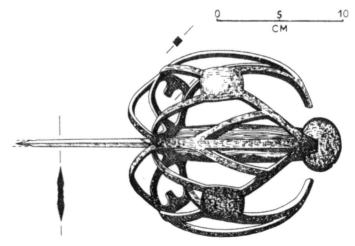

Smallsword. (Courtesy of the National Maritime Museum, *Naval Swords: British and American Naval Edged Weapons 1660 – 1815* by P.G.W. Annis)

In England, by the eighteenth century the use of smallswords eclipsed that of broadswords.[28] Developed between 1650 and 1720, the smallsword was light with a short, stiff blade and a simple, slender hilt. The art of fencing directly affected smallsword evolution; by 1660, French fencing masters arguing that speed was essential in swordplay, advocated a lighter, shorter blade than the rapier or broadsword.[29] They felt there was no longer a need for complicated guards or matching daggers with their new fencing style. Originally, the cross section of the blade was hexagonal, then diamond shaped, and finally triangular. These changes occurred as the smallsword evolved from cutting (no skill) to cut-and-thrust (minimal skill) to thrusting (advanced skill), reflecting the increasing sophistication of the techniques needed to wield it.[30]

The British smallsword hilt consisted at first of a plain shell guard (a popular guard shape on cutlasses of the latter half of the seventeenth and early eighteenth centuries consisting of an upturned guard encompassing the user's entire hand and scalloped in the shape of a shell), a straight grip, and a small knuckle guard. It had many decorations including the British Royal Cipher or crown, arms (pikes, muskets, axes, etc.), patriotic symbols such as eagles or lions, oak leaves, and floral or geometric designs. Excavators of the HM Brig *DeBraak* have even uncovered a pommel engraved with a fouled anchor design.

Smallsword pommel recovered from the wreck of HM Brig *DeBraak*. (Delaware State Museum)

Portrait of Lord Edward Hawke with smallsword. (Virginia Historical Society)

Eighteenth-century hilt ornamentation on a smallsword. (Dover Pictorial Archives Series)

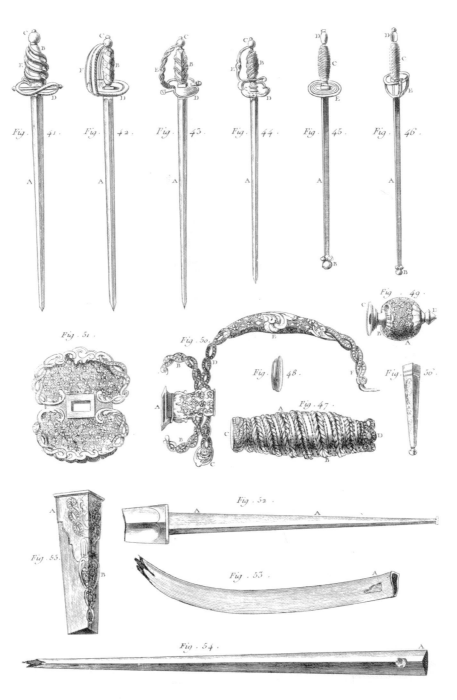

In America, the smallsword had a limited presence before 1688.[31] This absence was due mainly to the fact that the colonies were still developing a weapons industry. Many blacksmiths lacked the tools and artistic skills to produce swords equal to those available in Europe. Therefore, they created swords similar in style and shape to English smallswords, but distinguished by their simplicity.

Although army officers had carried hangers since the end of the fifteenth century, it was not until the eighteenth that they became popular in the

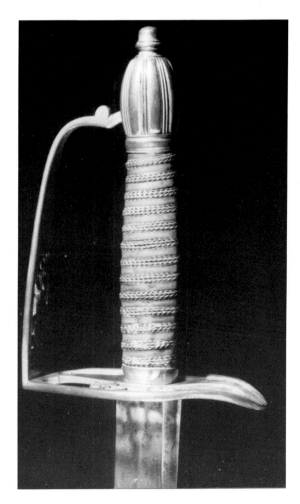

Slotted hilt of Commodore Matthew C. Perry's fighting sword. (Annapolis Naval Academy Collection)

Royal Navy.[32] A hanger was a light sabre with a single-edged blade, either curved or straight, and about 20in (50cm) long. Most hilts had a short, down-curving quillon with a small shell guard and a single knuckle bow. During the Revolutionary War, officers of the Royal Navy carried a slotted hilt hangar with an open-bar brass guard encircling a St. Edwards Crown over a fouled anchor. The grip was made of vertically fluted wood, and the blade was single-edged with a flat back and two fullers. Another popular style was the slotted hilt with anchor insets on the knuckle bow and guard. The grip and pommel were similar in design to the small sword with a fluted olive pommel and wire bound grip. Its small size made the hanger suitable as a naval weapon during the eighteenth century when England's naval and maritime commercial power was growing. Americans favoured the hanger from the seventeenth through the eighteenth centuries

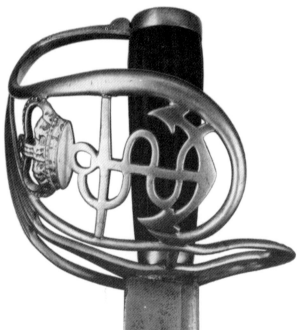

British slotted-hilt hanger favoured by officers of the Royal Navy during the American Revolution. (Courtesy of the National Maritime Museum, *Naval Swords: British and American Naval Edged Weapons 1660 – 1815* by P.G.W. Annis)

until the cutlass replaced it around 1780.[33]

Throughout the seventeenth and eighteenth centuries, men of the Royal Navy and the English colonists used a number of different cutting swords, most notably the cutlass. The term cutlass was derived from the French word *coutelas*, meaning 'large knife'.[34] In the documentary record, historians often encounter the names cutlasses, cutilax, curtle axe, coutelace, coutel axe, coutilas, cutlash or cutlace in reference to these weapons.[35] They are not the better-known cutlasses of the eighteenth and nineteenth centuries, however. The hanger, for example, is also referred to as a cutlass, as was any short, cut-and-thrust sword.[36] It was not until the eighteenth and nineteenth centuries that the term cutlass became exclusively associated with sabres used at sea, even though the Royal Navy simply listed them as 'swords for sea service'.[37]

Cutting swords had short, generally single-edged blades with a fuller that ran half the length. Hilts, on the other hand, evolved continually in order to protect the user's hand more effectively. Swords excavated at Plymouth, Massachusetts, have large, heavy pommels made of iron, with a knuckle bow that branched out on either side of the blade to form the counterguard. From the 1650s until the 1750s, the colonists also used a cutting sword with a horn grip and shell guard.[38]

By the middle of the eighteenth century, the Royal Navy had developed distinctive weapons as a direct result of the rise of naval professionalism.[39] By the end of the century, officers commonly carried lion- or eagle-head pommels with the smaller blade of the hanger and decorated with some type of nautical emblem. It was not long before eagle-head pommels appeared in America, but the patriotic symbolism attached to them today was not present

initially. The enlisted men of both navies continued to carry swords with heavy cutting blades and enclosed hilts.[40]

* * *

By the eighteenth century, firearms began to play a more important role in both naval and terrestrial battles. Neither the American nor the Royal Navy, however, abandoned the use of swords, axes, and polearms. Naval opponents fought battles from a distance with artillery, but once the conflict became closer, they needed hand-to-hand weapons due to the time constraints of reloading early firearms. Axes remained an effective tool and weapon for the navy and the colonists, including those who served in the militia. Polearms had all but disappeared from use in land battles by the 1790s but continued in use at sea for another century. The use of swords as personal protection and status symbol resonating with symbolic connotations assured their continued use. These early weapons, used in the Royal Navy and brought to America by the English colonists, were influential in the designs used by both navies in the next century.

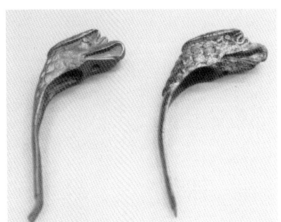

Examples of eighteenth-century eagle-head pommels. (Author's collection)

Edged Weapons of Enlisted Men in the Royal and American Navies, 1793–1865

From 1793 to 1865, enlisted men in the Royal Navy used edged weapons in a variety of wars including the Napoleonic Wars with France (1793–1815), the War of 1812 with the United States (1812–15), the First (1839–42) and Second (1856–60) Opium Wars with China, and the Crimean War with Russia (1854–6). Enlisted men in the US Navy used edged weapons for personal protection and in boarding actions during the Quasi-War with France (1791–1800), the Tripolitan war with the Barbary powers (1801–05), the War of 1812 with Britain, and the American Civil War (1861–5). These wars, fought on both land and sea, helped solidify Britain's naval power and establish America's. Weapon patterns used by both navies during this period fall into two periods (1793–1815 and 1840–65), when single vessels engaged in skirmishes that included the use of boarding axes, pikes and cutlasses. An analysis of these weapons provides a better understanding of the men who used them, and their capabilities and uses in naval warfare.

Enlisted men's weapons 1793–1815

In February 1793 Britain entered into a series of three wars with France commonly known collectively as the Napoleonic Wars (1793–1815). This conflict waged on land and sea would conclude more than a century of strife between the two countries, and establish the Royal Navy as the strongest and most influential naval power in the world. For 22 years, the navy was engaged in almost continual warfare in which it destroyed or captured 1201 enemy ships (712 French, 172 Dutch, 196 Spanish, 85 Danish, 4 Russian, 15 Turkish, and 17 American).[1] British

STATE OF THE ROYAL NAVY 1793–1816

Rate	1793	1804	1815	1816
Ships of the Line				
First Rates (100–120 guns)	5	7	10	9
Second Rates (90–98 guns)	19	15	12	14
Third Rates (64–80 guns)	114	129	169	150
Fourth Rates (50–60 guns)	22	20	17	17
Fifth Rates (32–44 guns)	90	128	167	147
Sixth Rates (20–28 guns)	41	33	47	42
Smaller vessels (sloops, brigs, etc)	99	291	419	364
Total	**390**	**623**	**841**	**743**

success was not due to technological or numerical superiority but rather the combined result of superior tactics and exceptional naval leadership.

By 1814 the Napoleonic Wars were coming to an end and Britain was able to direct its full force towards the war with the United States. Before long most American ships had either been captured or blockaded in harbour, and on 24 December 1814, the two countries signed a treaty ending all hostilities. The final action of the war, however, occurred on 8 January 1815 when Andrew Jackson defeated the British at the Battle of New Orleans.

STATE OF THE UNITED STATES NAVY DURING THE WAR OF 1812[2]

Rate	1812
Ships of the Line	
First Rates (100–120 guns)	0
Second Rates (90–98 guns)	0
Third Rates (64–80 guns)	3
Fourth Rates (50–60 guns)	0
Fifth Rates (32–44 guns)	11
Sixth Rates (20–28 guns)	3
Sloop of War (18 guns)	8
Brigs & Schooners (10–16 guns)	9
Ships on the Great Lakes (14–44 guns)	12
Total	**46**

Naval warfare in the early nineteenth century had changed little from that of the Revolutionary War period. In the Royal Navy, the ship's gunner was in charge of the care and distribution of arms and a certain portion of every crew were designated as boarders. HMS *Macedonian*, a 38-gun frigate, had 152 boarders (4 per gun crew) in a crew of 300 (about 50 per cent).[3] Out of this, 76 crewmembers were designated First Boarders and armed with cutlass and pistol. They were responsible for offensive action.

Next were the Second Boarders, 57 men armed with pikes and 19 with axes. Their initial responsibility was defensive in nature. The *Macedonian* also had 30 to 40 Marines designated to assist the Second Boarders if needed. The American Navy followed a similar method of boarder designation.[4]

When battle was imminent, the captain called for all hands to clear the ship for action. Samuel Leech, a sailor in the Royal Navy described this process as HMS *Macedonian* prepared to engage the *United States* on 25 October 1812:

A whisper ran along the crew that the stranger ship was a Yankee frigate. The thought was confirmed by the command of 'All hands clear the ship for action, ahoy!' The drum and fife [transverse flute] beat to quarters; bulk-heads were knocked away; the guns were released from their confinement; the whole dread paraphernalia of battle produced; and after the lapse of a few minutes of hurry and confusion, every man and boy was at his post, ready to do his best service for his country....[5]

While the ship was being prepared for action, the gunner's locker, which contained all boarding weapons, was opened. On board American vessels, boarding weapons were stored over each gun port as shown by the wreck of the naval schooner *Scourge* where after 192 years most weapons are still in place.[6] Leech continued his narration, describing how, when each man was at his post, 'A lieutenant then passed through the ship, directing the marines and boarders, who were furnished with pikes, cutlasses, and pistols, how to proceed if it should be necessary to board the enemy.'[7]

After the gunner distributed firearms, the crew received axes and pikes. The versatility of the axe increased in the eighteenth century as various forms of dismantling shot came into existence. During the course of a sea battle, enemy fire could bring down masts and rigging, putting the ship at risk.[8] If a mast fell along with other debris on the deck, the ship could not manoeuvre, making it an easy target and leaving it almost certain to be boarded or blown apart by an opponent's fire. HMS *Guerrière* had to surrender to USS *Constitution* after dismantling shot cut down *Guerrière*'s masts, damaging its hull, and injuring most of the crew.[9]

Throughout the fleet actions of the late eighteenth and early nineteenth centuries, the Royal Navy rarely used boarding as the principal route to victory. Some notable exceptions, however, included Commodore Horatio Nelson's capture of the Spanish ships *San Josef* (known at the time as the *San José*) and *San Nicholas* at the Battle of Cape St Vincent in February 1797. Nelson later described the action:

> *I directed Captain Miller to put the helm hard-a-starboard, and calling for the Borders, ordered them to Board. The soldiers of the 69th regiment, with an alacrity which will ever do them credit, were among the foremost on this service. The first man who jumped into the enemy's mizzen chains was Captain Berry, late my first lieutenant (Captain Miller was in the very act of going also, but I directed him to remain). A soldier having broke the upper quarter-gallery window, jumped in followed by myself and others as fast as possible. I found the cabin doors fastened, and some Spanish officers fired their pistols; but having broken open the doors, the soldiers fired, and the Spanish Brigadier fell as retreating to the quarter-deck. Having pushed on the quarter-deck, I found Captain Berry in possession of the poop, and the Spanish Ensign hauling down. The* San Josef *at this moment fired muskets and pistols from the Admiral's stern-gallery on us.*

> *Our seamen by this time were in full possession of every part: about seven of my men were killed, and some few wounded, and about twenty Spaniards.*

> *Having placed sentinels at the different ladders, and ordered Captain Miller to push more men into the* San Nicolas, *I directed my brave fellows to board the First-Rate, which was done in a moment.*[10]

Nelson's strategy of using one conquered ship to cross over with a boarding party from his flagship to a second enemy vessel became known in the Royal Navy as 'Nelson's Patent Bridge for Boarding First Rates'.

Boarding was more common in single-ship actions, one extraordinary Royal Navy example being the victory of the brig *Speedy* (14 guns), commanded by Lord Cochrane with 54 men, over the Spanish xebec-frigate *El Gamo* (32) with a crew of more than 300. On the morning of 6 May 1801 the *Speedy* was cruising off the coast of Barcelona when it encountered the powerful Spanish frigate. Outnumbered and outgunned, Cochrane made the bold and astonishing decision to engage the Spanish warship. The men quickly cleared for action. An efficient crew could do this in five minutes or so. The gunner handed out firearms and edged weapons as the men then manned their stations. They then waited until the two ships were within firing range of each other. The *El Gamo* fired the first shots before raising the Spanish flag. Cochrane, however, ran up an American flag to cause uncertainty and hesitation amongst the officers of the Spanish ship; this gave him enough time to sail up alongside, when he hoisted his real colours and began the action.

For the next few hours the two ships fired upon each other as the Spanish attempted unsuccessfully to board the *Speedy* three times. Meanwhile, Cochrane resolved to board the *El Gamo* and addressed his crew stating that they must, 'either take the frigate or be themselves taken, in which case the Spaniards would give no quarter'. Cochrane then led nearly all of *Speedy*'s crew, with faces blackened and cutlasses drawn, on to the deck of the *El Gamo*. According to Cochrane's own account, when the Spanish realised how few their attackers were they rallied, but Cochrane then called for another (non-existent) 50 boarders and the demoralised Spaniards surrendered.

During the War of 1812 the United States Navy was heavily outnumbered, but won a number of single-ship engagements with the British, although the American victories usually depended on superior firepower rather than boarding. In fact, when facing defeat at the hands of the USS *Constitution*, the British captains of the frigates *Guerrière* and *Java* had both attempted to save the day by boarding, but in each case were repulsed by the Americans. The only action in which the British successfully boarded an American frigate was the *Shannon*'s capture of USS *Chesapeake* in 1813, where the two ships were still engaged in a fierce gunnery duel when Captain Broke led his men onto his

NOTABLE NAVAL ACTIONS INFLUENCED BY EDGED WEAPONS 1793–1815

Vessels*	Date
HMS *Nymphe* (36) vs. *Cléopatre* (40)	18 Jun 1793
Antelope packet (6) vs. *Atalante* (8)	1 Dec 1793
HMS *Thorn* (16) vs. *Courier-National* (18)	25 May 1795
HMS *Captain* (74) vs. *San Nicolas* (80)	2 Feb 1797
HMS *Captain* (74) vs. *San Josef* (112)	2 Feb 1797
HMS *Mars* (74) vs. *Hercule* (74)	21 Apr 1798
Bayonnaise (28) vs. HMS *Ambuscade* (32)	14 Dec 1798
HMS *Wolverine* (12) vs. *Furet* (14) & *Rusé* (8)	12 Sep 1799
HMS *Surprize* (28) vs. *Hermione* (32)	25 Oct 1799
HMS *Viper* (14) vs. *Le Furet* (14)	26 Dec 1799
HMS *Dart* (30) vs. *Desiree* (36)	7 Jul 1800
HMS *Netley* (16) vs. *San Miguel* (9)	7 Nov 1800
HMS *Speedy* (14) vs. *El Gamo* (32)	6 May 1801
HMS *San Fiorenzo* (36) vs. *Psyché* (32)	13 Feb 1805
HMS *Pasley* (16) vs. *Virgen Del Rosario* (10)	27 Jul 1801
Ville de Milan (40) vs. *Cleopatra* (32)	16 Feb 1805
Windsor Castle packet vs. *Jeune Richard*	1 Oct 1807
Palinure (16) vs. HMS *Carnation* (18)	3 Oct 1808
HMS *Amethyst* (36) vs. *Thétis* (40)	10 Nov 1808
USS *Wasp* (18) vs. HMS *Frolic* (18)	18 Oct 1812
USS *Constitution* (44) vs. HMS *Java* (38)	29 Dec 1812
HMS *Shannon* (38) vs. USS *Chesapeake* (38)	1 Jun 1813
USS *Wasp* (18) vs. HMS *Reindeer* (18)	28 Jun 1814

*In each case the first named was the victor.

opponent's deck. Broke was struck down by the butt of a musket, but the American Captain Lawrence had already been mortally wounded and the leaderless American crew soon surrendered.

Axes

Between 1793 and 1815, the Board of Ordnance commissioned local cutlers in Birmingham, Sheffield and London to manufacture axes for the navy, though individual vessels would contract local smiths to make axes when in port for provisions. During the late eighteenth and early nineteenth centuries, the Royal Navy used two types of boarding axes. Although it was declining in popularity, the navy continued to use the tomahawk-style boarding axe that had been used for over a century. By the 1790s, however, a modified pattern appeared. Instead of the rounded head of previous models, the new axe had a broad, square head measuring between 9 and 12in (22.8 and 30.4cm) long, and ⅛in (3mm) thick. The downward-curving spike poll was maintained, but was shortened considerably to equal only a quarter of the length of the head. Lobe-shaped langets secured the head to a round-butted ash staff. Each axe had a diamond-shaped metal plaque nailed to the staff, which was stamped with identification markings such as 'R3'.

During and after the American Revolution, the US Navy commonly used a rounded tomahawk-style boarding axe acquired from captured British stores.[11] By the 1790s, however, a distinctive American axe appeared, produced by local manufacturers such as Henry Foxall and Robert Gill of Baltimore, Maryland as well as blacksmiths in Philadelphia.[12] The round axe head was revolutionary because of the addition of teeth to the heel of the blade, which proved most effective in hooking and dragging fallen rigging across the deck.

By studying personal correspondence and ship

British boarding axe from the period 1750–1850. (Courtesy of N. Flayderman & Co., *Small Arms of the Sea Services* by Colonel Robert H. Rankin)

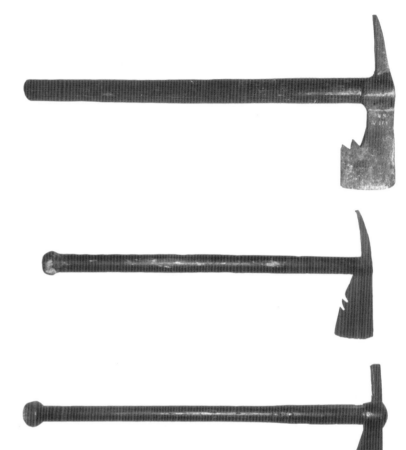

American boarding axes from the period 1800–10 (top), 1800–20 (middle), and 1820–40 (bottom). (Courtesy of N. Flayderman & Co., *Small Arms of the Sea Services* by Colonel Robert H. Rankin)

manifests, it is possible to determine not only the number of axes carried on British and American vessels, but also how many were issued to members of the crew. The number of axes allocated to a vessels of the Royal Navy generally equalled anywhere from a quarter to double the number of guns. A 74-gun ship by 1797, for example, carried 100 axes, or about one for every six crewmembers. Generally this ratio equated to enough axes for 11–17 per cent of the crew.

In a letter dated August 1797, James McHenry wrote to Wm. John Harris requesting 100 boarding axes to outfit the USS *Constitution* (44).[13] The

Constitution was one of six frigates ordered by Congress for the new federal navy in 1794. It carried a crew of roughly 450 men, so 22 per cent of the crew would have been issued an axe. Later that year, McHenry requested another 100 boarding axes for the 36-gun frigate *Constellation* (44).[14] Vessels carrying less then 44 guns generally carried only 20 axes, or enough for 5 to 10 per cent of the crew.[15]

On board British and American vessels, axes were stored on racks most of the time. When individually carried, a leather scabbard-like sheath was used to protect the blade. The top, however, was open to allow easy withdrawal. The handle protruded through an opening in the bottom of the sheath.[16]

Today there are few surviving specimens of boarding axes to examine, especially compared to swords. In all of the major museums of the world, one can scarcely find a boarding axe from this period. This may be, in part, because boarding axes would have been amongst the last tools or weapons on the list of priorities scheduled for replacement. They were utilitarian objects, relatively static in their evolution compared to swords, and unlike pikes, were useful even after boarding became an impractical tactic. These reasons led to a much longer life span for shipboard axes, which may have been used until they were worn out and then thrown away.

Given that axes were tools issued to ships not individuals, most carry only identification marks. Axes used by the Royal Navy were commonly marked only with the Crown's broad arrow, production number or storage location. American axes, on the other hand were stamped with 'U.S. Navy', an inspector's marks and the manufacturer's initials on the face of the blade. The most commonly found marks of this period are: 'U.S./ V.IM,' 'U.S./N.Y.W,' or 'U.S./ Hoffman.' The 'V.IM' proof mark indicates that John McLean,

Axes still in place onboard the wreck of the *Scourge*. (Courtesy of The *Hamilton* and *Scourge* Project)

Commissary of Military Stores for the State of New York, inspected the axe; 'N.Y.W' (Navy Yard Washington) is the manufacturer's mark for the Washington, D.C. Navy Yard; and 'Hoffman' refers to an 1806 Philadelphia blade maker who produced axes for the American Navy.[17]

Pikes

As with axes, the use of pikes by land forces ended in the early eighteenth century, but survived another 200 years at sea. They differed from the traditional terrestrial pike in several respects. First, manufacturers did not cover the butt of the handle in metal because it would damage the deck; they made the butt in the shape of a ball or left it rounded. Second, boarding pikes were never as long as those used on land. The average infantry pike ranged between 16 and 18ft (4.9 and 5.5m) in length, while boarding

Pike butts. (Courtesy of
N. Flayderman & Co.,
*American Polearms 1526-
1865: The Lance,
Halberd, Spontoon, Pike
and Naval Boarding
Weapons* by Rodney
Hilton Brown)

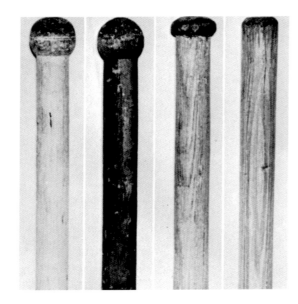

Pike butts. (Courtesy of N. Flayderman & Co., *American Polearms 1526-1865: The Lance, Halberd, Spontoon, Pike and Naval Boarding Weapons* by Rodney Hilton Brown)

version, which land forces had used for almost 200 years. Square or triangular in section, it was limited to only thrusting, requiring little skill or training to handle. Although not as commonly used in the Royal Navy as the pick-style, many vessels carried a leaf-bladed pike. The head measured between 10 and 13in (25.4 and 33cm) in length with a diamond cross-section, which could be used for cutting as well as thrusting. The cylindrical base was 3 to 4in (7.6 to 10.1cm) in length and continued down to form two langets that attached to the sides of the staff. Both types of pikes had ash hafts, and contained a leather sheath secured with a heavy white cord to protect the head from damage while stored.[19]

Diamond-shaped pike head. (Annapolis Naval Academy Collection)

pikes were generally around 12ft (3.7m). The half-pike was around 8ft (2.4m), and the quarter-pike was only 4ft (1.2m) in length. The reduced size was preferred for the confined quarters of a ship. They were simple in design and had no embellishments, so sailors would not accidentally get them caught in the rigging while repelling boarders.

From 1793 to 1815, there were no strict regulations regarding boarding pikes, and the Royal Navy used two basic styles. Francis Bannerman listed British boarding pikes for $3.85 each in his *Surplus Military Weapons Catalog*, describing the first style as:

> … *4½ inch three sided pike blade with 10-inch iron straps, fastened to hard wood pole. Full length 7½ feet, diameter 1¼ inches. Some of the pikes have lozenge shaped brass plate with number so that each sailor could identify his own pike. … Similar pikes used on board old wooden frigates of U.S. Navy.*[18]

The pick-style was adapted from the infantry

Leaf-shaped pike head. (Annapolis Naval Academy Collection)

Little documentary evidence survives to indicate the pike style preferred by the US Navy in the late eighteenth century. In 1797, the War Department had new patterns drawn for several small arms, and according to William Gilkerson, the evidence of the artefacts suggests that the pike favoured was a leaf-bladed version similar to that used by the Royal Navy. The full length was 95in (2.4m), with a four-sided spearhead 7in (17.9cm) long and held in place on the staff with iron langets painted entirely white.[20]

Between 1793 and 1815, the US Navy ordered

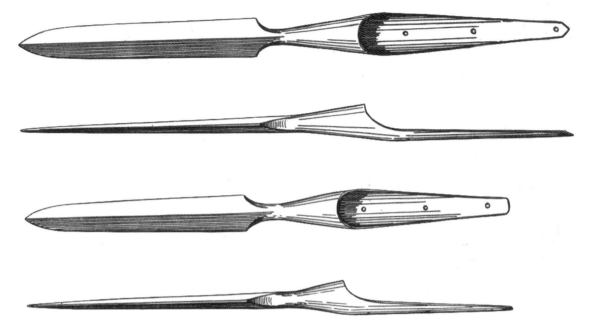

Model 1816 boarding pike produced by Nathan Starr. (Courtesy of Andre Jandot)

massive amounts of boarding weapons. In a letter dated June 1797, John Harris requested from Samuel Hodgdon 300 boarding pikes to outfit three frigates. In November, he wrote again, requesting 100 boarding or quarter-pikes each for the USS *Constitution* and *Constellation*.[21] Another known manufacturer of pikes was Nathan Starr, to whom the government awarded a pike contract in 1815. Already renowned for his swords, he was commissioned to produce 1000 boarding pikes at a cost of 75 cents each.[22]

As with axes, the number of boarding pikes allocated to vessels of the Royal Navy roughly correlated to the number of guns it carried. A 74-gun ship carried 60 pikes, or about one for every 10 crewmembers in 1797. Generally this ratio provided enough pikes for about 10 per cent of the crew or about one pike per gun crew. Based on ship manifests and contracts, it seems that in vessels of the US Navy the numbers of pikes carried depended their gun rating – usually between 50 (for ships of less than 64 guns) and 100 (64–100 guns).[23] As with all small arms, pikes were under the care and responsibility of the gunner, so presumably were normally kept in the gunner's store aboard Royal Navy vessels,[24] although when going into action they were usually arrayed vertically in racks encircling the masts. On American vessels, they were similarly ready to hand – for example, on the wreck of the *Scourge* pikes were attached to the main boom.

Pikes from this period are scarce today, due in part to iron shortages when polearms would be re-forged.[25] Out of those that have survived, all are stamped with some type of identification mark on the head. British pikes are marked with the Crown's broad arrow or with '2↑0'. American pikes are marked with the place of manufacture or an inspector's mark. Among these marks are 'U.S./N.Y.W' (Navy Yard Washington), 'U.S./HHP/P' indicating inspection by Henry H. Perkins, or simply 'U.S.'.

Cutlasses

Unlike axes or pikes, the cutlass is the traditional weapon associated with the enlisted man. Even though antiquated, naval vessels carried them until the Second World War.[26] When the Admiralty commissioned HMS *Warrior* in 1861, an iron-hulled steamship, which made the prospect of boarding slim, provisions were still made for pikes and cutlasses. Similarly, the *Albemarle*, a Confederate ironclad of the Civil War era, had cutlass racks onboard.

Cutlasses played an important role in the protection of a ship, and were the enlisted sailor's preferred weapon in both the Royal and US navies. Designed as cutting and thrusting weapons, anyone could use them regardless of skill or training, which enlisted men did not officially or regularly receive in the eighteenth century.[27] By 1815, both navies realised the need for regular weapon training amongst the enlisted men, many of which had never handled a sword before entering the service. Onboard the USS *Essex*, for example, men were exercised daily with boarding weapons. David Farragut, who served under Captain David Porter onboard the *Essex* during the War of 1812, and was later a distinguished American naval officer in his own right, wrote:

> *…I have never been on board a ship where the crew of the old* Essex *was represented but that I found them to be the best swordsmen on board. They had been so thoroughly trained as boarders that every man was prepared for such an emergency, with his cutlass as sharp as a razor* …[28]

The general cutlass used between 1793 and 1815 had a short blade and a large knuckle bow. The shorter blade was preferred since it did not hinder a man when climbing rigging or when swinging from one ship to another. It was also more effective in the confined spaces of a warship where little space was available for hand-to-hand combat. Sailors preferred the larger knuckle guard because it provided more protection from cuts that could take a man's hand off.

During this stage of weapon development, the Royal Navy issued three cutlass models for enlisted men. The first, designed by London cutler Thomas Hollier in the early eighteenth century, was still in use a hundred years later. Hollier's cutlass consisted of a rounded, disk-shaped knuckle guard with a second disk guard or figure-of-eight style. The blade had an average length of 28in (71cm).

Cutlass hilt designed by Thomas Hollier in the early eighteenth century. (Courtesy of Ray Riling Arms Books Co., *The American Sword 1775–1945*, by Harold Peterson)

In 1804 Henry Osborn suggested a new and improved cutlass pattern to the Board of Ordnance, which they accepted in May of that year. The new cutlass had a straighter and shorter blade than the previous model, with black iron mounts added, and lacked the fullers found on previous model. The M1804 was heavier and bulkier in response to the sailor's need for a stronger weapon with more protection for the user's hand. Osborn enlarged the knuckle bow into one disk instead of the previous two, thereby providing more coverage. Furthermore, instead of making the grip smooth and straight as previously done, the grip was corrugated to improve the user's grasp and reduce the risk of slipping during battle.

In May 1804 the Board of Ordnance ordered 10,000 Osborn cutlasses at a cost of 4/10d each, and another 20,000 in 1808 at a cost of 4/6d each.[29] Manufacturers other then Henry Osborn produced this new pattern including James Woolley, Thomas Craven, T. Hadley, Samuel Dawes, George Reddell, John Cooper and Thomas Bates. Daniel Frazer and James Esdaile & Company manufactured and the scabbards separately.

BOARDING CUTLASSES ORDERED BY THE ROYAL NAVY 1804–08 [30]

Manufacturer	Number ordered
James Woolley & Co.	5150
Thomas Craven	1750
Henry Osborn	5600
T. Hadley	1750
Samuel Dawes	4950
Thomas Gill	3400
Thomas Hadley	2500
George Reddell	2000
John Cooper	1500
Thomas Bates	1400
Total	**30,000**

In 1814 the Board of Ordnance decided that the M1804 cutlass was not as efficient a weapon as they had hoped and discarded it in favour of a cup-guard model, similar to that used by the US Navy.[31] Designed and submitted by the sword cutlers Tatham & Egg, the M1814 had a modified guard and blade. The knuckle bow was similar to the 1804 design, but enlarged slightly. The blade, on the other hand, was completely changed. It was shorter, wider and more curved than past models, with a fuller restored on one side to lighten and strengthen the blade. This style proved so effective that the Royal Navy did not contract a new cutlass design until 1841.[32] Unlike axes and pikes, the number of swords allocated to a vessel in the Royal Navy was more than double the number of guns carried, so that 39 per cent of the crew was armed with swords, or equivalent to three swords per gun crew.

The first American naval cutlasses appeared in the 1770s when the Continental Navy ordered them for use during the American Revolution.[33] They had double-edged blades 16in (40.6cm) in length, 1⅛in (2.8cm) in width. Sam Morris, Andrew Hodge, Francis Clark and Josiah Wood were the principal Philadelphia manufacturers.[34] From 1755 to 1790 cutlasses were also obtained from Philadelphia companies owned by William York and John Pringle,

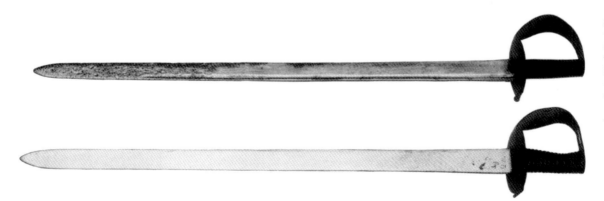

English cutlasses of the 1790s (top) and 1804 (bottom). (Courtesy of the National Maritime Museum, *Naval Swords: British and American Naval Edged Weapons 1660–1815*, by P.G.W. Annis.)

who obtained blades from the cutlers of Solingen, Germany.[35]

By 1798 French privateers posed a growing threat to American shipping routes in the Caribbean. To deal with this problem, the government established the Congressional Act (or Army Bill) of April 1798 to provide additional armament for vessels that protected American commerce. The government increased the navy by purchasing, building or hiring 12 additional small warships.[36]

To arm this growing fleet, contracts were awarded to Nathan Starr of Middletown, Connecticut, to produce the needed cutlasses. He not only became the first official manufacturer of American naval swords, but he also received national recognition for the quality of the blades he produced. The Starr cutlass was patterned after those used by the Royal Navy with some minor variations. Whereas the British cutlass had a corrugated iron grip, its American counterpart had a smooth cylindrical iron or wooden grip reminiscent of Hollier's cutlass.[37] The overall length was between 28 and 33in (71 and 83.8cm). The blade averaged between 25 and 28in (63.5 and 71cm) in length, and 1½in (3.8cm) in width. It was single-edged and contained a solitary fuller that terminated 6in (15.2cm) from the point. The knuckle bow was a simple flat strip of iron with two elliptical lobes on either side that narrowed into a roughly circular counterguard similar to the M1804. The quillon terminated in a simple curl slightly above the blade.

BOARDING AXES, PIKES & CUTLASSES ORDERED BY THE AMERICAN NAVY

Vessel	Number Ordered			Date
	Pikes	Axes	Cutlasses	
Crescent	50	—	50	Jun 1797
Constitution	100	100	100	Nov 1797
Constellation	100	100	150	Nov 1797
United States	100	100	100	Apr 1798
Ganges	6	10	—	May 1798
General Greene	—	20	10	May 1798
United States	76	100	100	May 1798
Delaware	—	—	10	Jun 1798
2 Galleys	50	—	—	Aug 1798
Norfolk	60	—	—	Aug 1798
Herald	12	—	20	Sep 1798
Adams	100	—	100	Apr 1799
Maryland	100	—	—	Jun 1799
Essex	100	—	100	Jun 1799
President	—	100	—	May 1800
New York	—	100	—	May 1800
Total	**854**	**630**	**740**	

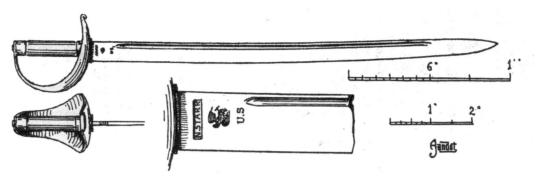

Model 1808 naval cutlass produced by Nathan Starr. (Courtesy of Andre Jandot)

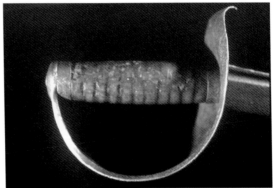

Cutlass hilt produced by Nathan Starr. (Annapolis Naval Academy Collection)

In 1808 the American Navy contracted Starr to produce a new style of cutlass. As with the British M1814, the pattern developed was so effective that the US Navy did not commission another cutlass pattern until the 1840s. They ordered 2000 M1808 swords at a cost of $2.50 each.[38] The overall length was set at 35in (88.9cm). The grip was a simple maple cylinder with an iron ferrule at each end. The pommel was flat and formed by the end of the knuckle guard, which terminated in a slight curl above the blade. The blade was straight except for a slight curve towards the tip, single-edged, and contained a fuller that terminated 4in (10.1cm) from the point. The blade length remained at 28in (71cm), but the width was decreased to 1in (2.5cm). Starr made this alteration to the blade so sailors could use it as an effective cutting or thrusting weapon. These changes were significant as they reflected the US Navy's movement towards building a more professional corps of sailors that would need to be skilled in the handling of weapons at sea.

American historians call the period from 1799 until 1826 the Starr Era because of the large number of cutlasses he supplied to the navy.[39] As a result, his cutlass is often described as the norm, but it would be erroneous to assume that Starr was the only manufacturer, or that his cutlass was the only style used by the US Navy during a period that lacked any widespread standardisation of naval edged weapons.

Lewis Prahl of Philadelphia and Robert Dingee of New York were amongst those who also produced weapons for the Navy Department.[40]

Between 1808 and 1826, Jacob S. Baker supplied a different type of cutlass to the navy. Like Starr however, his inspiration came from the weapons carried by the enlisted men in the Royal Navy. The overall length of the sword he manufactured was 34in (86.3cm), with a slightly curved blade 29in (73.6cm) long and 1in (2.5cm) wide. Like Hollier's weapon, it had no fullers. Baker produced the guard from a single sheet of iron to form a figure-of-eight pattern, and the hilt had the corrugate rosewood grip of the M1804.

In both Britain and America, the naval cutlass was strictly a utilitarian weapon. Sailors did not use them as dress items or badges of authority, and the government did not use them as a means of distin-

Figure '8' cutlass used by the American and Royal navies between the 1790s and the 1840s. (Annapolis Naval Academy Collection)

Cutlass still in place onboard the wreck of the *Scourge*. (Courtesy of The *Hamilton* and *Scourge* Project)

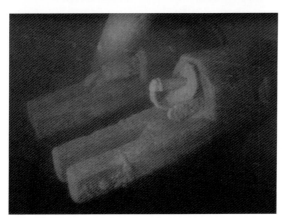

Cutlass still in place onboard the wreck of the *Hamilton*. (Courtesy of The *Hamilton* and *Scourge* Project)

guishing between the different ranks of sailors (able seamen, ordinary seaman and landsmen). Weapons were issued to specific vessels, not individuals and the men seldom had reason to purchase their own weapon. In 1806 a sailor in the Royal Navy earned between 22s 6d (£1.12.5p) and 33s 6d (£2.47.5p) per Lunar Month (28 days). To purchase a weapon would cost more than twice their annual pay.[41] The pay for US sailors was much better than their English counterparts at $10 to $12 dollars per month, which was as much or more than a skilled artisan on shore earned. A personal sword, however, would have cost a sailor almost a third or half of their annual salary.

The Board of Ordnance and the US Department of the Navy designed cutlasses, axes and pikes as weapons. Therefore, they were usually simple in design, lacking any type of ornamentation or decorative symbols, and stamped only with a manufacturer or inspector's mark. British cutlasses, for example, were marked with the royal cipher of King George III, a crown over a figure, or a broad arrow.[42] The American M1804 cutlass blade was also marked with viewer's marks indicating government inspection.

Royal cyphers on nineteenth-century British cutlasses. (Courtesy of the National Maritime Museum)

3   2   8   4

Viewer's marks on nineteenth-century British cutlasses. (Courtesy of the National Maritime Museum)

American cutlasses were commonly marked with manufacturer's name, eagles and roman numerals stamped on the blade. Swords manufactured between 1798 and 1815 are commonly marked with 'STARR /U.S.', or 'N STARR', a United States eagle and the letters 'U.S.' on the obverse.[43] Other blades are found stamped with names such as 'J.S. Baker' or 'PRAHL'. Some have roman numerals from 'I' to 'LXL' stamped on the spine, which were station numbers indicating where the weapon should be located on a vessel.[44] Similar to British viewer's marks, American cutlasses were marked with a 'P' as a sign of government inspection along with the inspector's initials such as 'HHP'.

Until 1806 both the British and American governments imported a large number of blades from Solingen, Germany, and numerous examples can be found today with the markings of Dominick Kirschbaum (1740), Abraham Stamm (1750) or J. J. Runkel (1780–1800) stamped on the blade.[45] As Napoleonic control spread across Europe in the first decade of the nineteenth century, the international blade trade became closed to Britain. Thereafter, the Royal Navy had to depend upon the blades produced domestically by cutlers at Shotley Bridge, Birmingham, London and Portsmouth.[46] The American government faced a similar dilemma after Napoleon invaded Germany and closed Solingen in 1806. Even after the factory reopened it was too busy filling government contracts to deal with outside orders. The US Navy then had to depend upon their own cutlers to acquire blades.

The eighteenth century, with its wars and revolutions, gave tremendous stimulus to the development of naval weapons. Recognisable edged weaponry that differed from terrestrial models appeared for the enlisted men as the concept of professionalism gathered strength. This happened first in the Royal Navy leading to the introduction of regulation patterns by the end of the Napoleonic War. During this period, the Royal Navy was busy re-outfitting their vessels with weapons that were more efficient than those used in previous decades. In America, the production of edged weapons also increased at this time, as the government continued building up their navy. The weapons used by the enlisted men and developed between 1793 and 1815 remained unchanged until the mid-nineteenth century in both the Royal and US Navies.

Enlisted men's weapons 1841–65

During the early nineteenth century, very little changed about the ships and tactics used by the Royal and US navies. For more than 200 years ships had fought upon essentially the same principles. Wooden ships such as ships-of-the-line, frigates and brigs fought with line-of-battle tactics and solid shot armament. The 20-year period between the 1840s and 1860s, however, was a time of rapid and extreme changes in naval technology, and more advances were made than had occurred in nearly a thousand years of previous naval history. Every aspect evolved, from ship construction to propulsion to ordnance. In many ways, the British and American navies had to start afresh to cope with these developments.

Changes to naval technology and administration during this period directly affected the design of edged weapons, how men were trained to use them, and – fundamentally – how they were used in battles at sea. It would be several more decades however, before they were rendered obsolete. Axes, pikes and cutlasses were still carried aboard vessels, and enlisted men were still drilled regularly. Officers still owned fighting and dress swords, and the symbolic significance placed on such weapons reached its apogee with US naval officers of the American Civil War period. Besides examining changing patterns in weaponry, it is important to examine the technological and administrative changes that impinged on weapons styles during this period.

By the 1840s the impact of the Industrial Revolution and the advent of steam brought about the dawn of a new era in naval warfare. In the following decades, novel forms of propulsion – first paddle-wheel steamers, then screw, and finally twin-screw propellers – replaced sailing vessels. Wind was no longer a factor, with the paddle wheel, but it left the means of propulsion vulnerable to enemy fire. Navies perceived submerged propellers as safer, and the British built the first, HMS *Rattler*, in 1843, followed closely by the US Navy's *Princeton*. Further technological advancements included rigging as it evolved from rope to wire, and sails were reduced in number until they were only an auxiliary means of propulsion.

In the era of sail, ship design was not so specialised and there was little difference between the naval architecture of warships and merchantmen. From the 1860s, however, a radical diversification of ships types began, as the forerunners of later battleships, cruisers, torpedo boats and the earliest forms of submarines appeared. There was a move towards iron rather than wood for hull construction during this period, iron hulls being generally stronger and less prone to 'working' (the distortions to wooden ships known as sagging, hogging, compressions, tension, etc.). As a percentage of displacement, iron hulls were lighter, promising greater carrying capacity (whether armament or cargo), and allowing a shallower draft, and more manoeuvrability. They were also more resistant to underwater damage – as was notably demonstrated when the *Great Britain* ran aground in 1846, remained there all winter, and was still usable when refloated in 1847.

Despite all these advantages, the United States still had a hard time accepting iron hulls. This situation was due in part to the country's vast natural resources of wood, which led the government to believe it would be unprofitable to turn to iron. Great Britain, on the other hand, with exhausted timber resources but a flourishing iron industry, had more incentive to adopt and improve this new technology. In the 1830s the true cost of iron fell, which made it an economic alternative to scarce shipbuilding timber, and the first iron-hulled warships were built in Britain in 1839–40.

To convert to iron hulls involved a great commitment by the government and shipping industry. There was the problem of transportation infrastructure, especially in the United States where ironworks were seldom near shipbuilding yards. The manufacturing of iron meant the introduction of mechanised equipment, which in turn required the conversion of skilled labour from shipwrights to machinists. Furthermore, iron-hulled vessels needed worldwide docking facilities because iron corroded easily, and because, at first, there was no effective method of anti-fouling. Finally, the US government placed tariffs on the importation of iron that protected the timber industry and held back iron production for decades.

As steam engines improved, propellers were developed and battle tactics gradually evolved from the centuries-old certainties of the line of battle. Changing tactics were part of a process that also involved radical improvements to ordnance, which progressed from solid round, grape and bar shot to explosive shells in ever-larger calibres, giving guns greater range, accuracy and effect. Furthermore, rifled breechloaders and smokeless powder replaced smoothbore guns and slow-burning black powder. As gun size and effectiveness increased, the need for armour became apparent; then the bigger the guns became, the thicker the armour became to counter the threat.

The history of the Royal Navy in the nineteenth century can be divided into roughly three phases. The first, lasting from 1815 to 1830, saw the culmination of the sailing warship. By 1830 major changes in hull forms and ordnance were occurring as well as the first stages of the introduction of steam propulsion. During this period the navy relied on a mixed fleet of sailing and steam vessels. By the third phase, beginning about 1852, screw propulsion had been accepted as an essential element of the future battle fleet, and pure sailing ships all but disappeared as a major factor in naval operations.

As the navy's order of battle evolved so too did its administration. Until the 1830s the Navy Board had formed a permanent bureaucracy, nominally answering to the politically-appointed Board of Admiralty, but often exerting its independence. However, in 1832 it was absorbed into the Admiralty to form a single organisation responsible for every aspect of the naval affairs of the nation. The Board of Ordnance, a separate government department, was responsible for the procurement of all weapons for both the army and navy. In 1840 George Lovell was appointed the Inspector of Small Arms and made responsible for the procurement of all the Royal Navy's edged weapons. By 1854, however, the office of the Board of Ordnance had been abolished and all responsibilities taken over by the War Office.

STATE OF THE ROYAL NAVY, 1845–60 [47]

In Commission	1845	1855	1860
Sailing Ships			
First Rates (110–120 guns)	6	8	3
Second Rates (80–100)	9	9	9
Third Rates (74–76)	1	0	0
Fourth Rates (50–60)	7	0	0
Fifth Rates (38–42)	5	10	0
Sixth Rates (28)	15	7	0
Sloops and other vessels	66	33	9
Steam Ships			
First Rates (101–131)	0	4	2
Second Rates (80–91)	0	12	34
Third Rates (60–70)	0	10	0
Screw Frigates	0	5	20
Paddle Frigates	4	17	7
Screw-Sloops	1	26	45
Paddle-Sloops	16	28	27
Paddle-Vessels	10	40	—
Screw Vessels	0	7	11
Steam Vessels	—	—	16
Total	**140**	**216**	**183**

In the years immediately following the end of the Napoleonic Wars, the Royal Navy experienced a rapid reduction in force strength. By 1820 the number of commissioned vessels had been reduced by 81.3 per cent, and manpower was cut from 90,000 in 1815 to 23,000 in 1820. While sailors and boys were discharged and sent ashore, 5017 officers were maintained on half pay. By the 1840s the Royal Navy was again building up its corps of enlisted men to face a series of missions and wars that would last through the 1860s. Although the navy never reached the numbers seen during the Napoleonic Wars the average strength of the navy in the 1840s was 39,866.5, followed by 54,748 in the 1850s and finally 70,788.2 in the 1860s.

In 1827 the last fleet action fought under sail occurred at the Battle of Navarino when a combined fleet of English/French/Russian ships commanded by Vice-Admiral Sir Edward Codrington destroyed the Turkish/Egyptian fleet, leading to the independence of Greece from Ottoman Turkey. Twelve years later, Britain was entangled in the first of two Opium Wars (1839–42 and 1856–60) with China. In between these conflicts, England and France fought the Russians in the Crimean War (1854–6). Edged weapons were carried aboard the vessels that served in these wars, and were used in small-scale boardings of Chinese junks during the Opium Wars and in capturing pirate and slave ships.

From the 1820s through the 1860s, vessels of the Royal Navy were used in the suppression of piracy on the high seas and on anti-slavery patrols. Commonly chasing single vessels, the Royal Navy had much more need of edged weapons and boarding tactics as an alternative means of capturing these elusive ships. In order to carry out their objectives of abolishing piracy and the slave trade, the Royal Navy maintained patrolling ships off the coasts of Africa, Brazil, and the Caribbean, as well as the Far East. The total number of vessels increased in size by almost five times from 1820 to 1840, and by 1848, the squadron included 34 cruisers stationed throughout the world.

By the late 1820s the Royal Navy realised that the method of training gun crews in the proper handling of weapons was erratic at best. Some ships trained their gun crews regularly, while others did not perform training at all. In 1829 Commander George Smith submitted a proposal to the Board of Admiralty for the creation of a proper school to train enlisted men. In 1830 the Board accepted his proposal and established a school in Portsmouth onboard HMS *Excellent* for the training of gun crews and the testing of new equipment. After 1857 the school was briefly moved to HMS *Illustrious*.

Each cadet received training on great guns, rifles and cutlasses as well as seamanship. In the 1850s the Admiralty published *The Seaman's Catechism* detailing cutlass exercises.[48] There were only four cuts and four guards. Two points were given from and parried by the guards: 'attention,' 'draw swords' (rear rank step back), 'slope swords', 'from right or left extend (prove distance with swords as they go)', 'take open order for exercise' (front rank cross the deck and face right about), 'prove distance' (all round from right rear to left front), and 'perform sword exercise' (raise the arm level the pommel at shoulder of man opposite carrying left foot to the rear and placing left arm behind the back). In both the Royal and American navies, men trained with single sticks. Used up to the 1920s, these practice weapons saved wear and tear on the metal blades of real cutlasses, as well as on the sailors using them. They typically consisted of an inch-wide, yard-long ash-wood stick that tapered toward the tip. Eighteenth-century single sticks had a basket-like guard ('pot') made of reed, but later versions were outfitted with triangular guards of stiff cow or buffalo hide.[49]

As with the Royal Navy, the United States experienced a series of dramatic changes in the years between the 1820s and 1860s. In 1815 the Board of Naval Commissioners was established to take on the tasks traditionally performed by the Secretary of the Navy. In 1816 Congress passed the Act for the Gradual Increase of the Navy. In this act, Congress voted $1 million for the construction of nine ships-of-the-line and twelve 44-gun frigates to be constructed over the course of eight years.[50]

In the decades between the War of 1812 and the Civil War, America experienced an unprecedented growth in maritime trade, accompanied by the rapid expansion of territory. To manage the growing navy and protect American commercial interests, a more efficient naval administration was called for but was much harder to achieve. By the beginning of the Civil War, the US Navy was wholly unprepared, and the Confederate states did not have a navy at all.

In 1855 six screw frigates composed the main strength of the Union's navy. Unfortunately, when war broke out they found themselves fighting an enemy which this type of vessel was unequipped to deal with. For the most part naval battles did not occur on the ocean, but rather in areas too shallow to permit large frigates. The Royal Navy had faced a similar dilemma when fighting the American colonists during the Revolutionary War.

VESSELS BELONGING TO THE UNION AND CONFEDERATE NAVIES, 1865[51]

Union	670
Confederate	130

Throughout the Civil War, both the Union and Confederate navies had difficulty in recruiting for their ships. In the Confederate Navy the shortage was severe enough for the Secretary of the Navy Stephen R. Mallory to ask the Confederate Congress to pass a law in 1863 allowing men to transfer from the army to the navy. Commerce raiders, such as the *Alabama*, *Florida* and *Shenandoah*, however, had no trouble in obtaining men through either the allure of riches or by impressment of men from captured ships.

CSS *Florida*. (Naval Historical Center)

CSS *Alabama*. (Naval
Historical Center)

CSS *Shenandoah*. (Naval
Historical Center)

ENLISTED MEN IN THE UNION AND CONFEDERATE NAVIES[52]

	1861	1865
Union	7600	51,000
Confederate	——	4000

Almost all sailors in both the Union and Confederate navies went to a receiving vessel to train in the everyday tasks of running a ship and fighting battles at sea. They would spend a large portion of their time learning how to handle their guns and in cutlass drill. Each man would be trained not only in how to board an enemy ship, but also how to repel an assault. Training on a receiving ship varied depending on the need for men, and could last anywhere from a few days to several weeks.

Although the advances in naval technology made boarding difficult, if not impossible, it remained an appealing alternative tactic for a navy that had neither the ships, armament nor men that its enemy did. Confederate raiders effectively used boarding as a means of winning battles against the better-equipped vessels of the Union Navy. In 1864 sailors of the Confederate Navy were able to launch a successful boarding operation against the *Water Witch*:

> *In May, last Lieutenant Commanding Thos. P. Pelot, under Flag-Officer Hunter's command at Savannah, organized a boat party against the enemy in Ossabaw Sound, and on the night of the 3d of June attacked, and after a desperate contest carried by boarding, the U. S. sloop Water Witch, Lieutenant-Commander Austin Pendergrast, U. S. Navy, of four guns, and a crew of 80 officers and men, with a loss to the enemy of 2 killed and 14 wounded. The enemy was not surprised, and had his crew at quarters and his boarding nettings up; and our loss was 6 killed and 17 wounded. In this gallant achievement the Navy lost one of its most accomplished officers in Lieutenant Pelot, who was killed at the head of his boarding party after gaining the enemy's deck.*[53]

In 1862, Stephen R. Mallory, Secretary of the Navy for the Confederacy, thought boarding was an

Cutlass drill.
(Author's collection)

'excellent means of taking an ironclad vessel'.[54] He felt that rowboats, barges, and small steamers could take a larger vessel by boarding if they attacked two or three at a time. Boarders should be divided into parties of tens and twenties, under a separate leader: one party with iron wedges to jam between the turret and the deck; a second to cover the pilothouse with wet blankets; a third threw powder down the smoke stack; another group provided with turpentine or camphene in glass vessels to smash over the turret to produce inextinguishable liquid fire; and a final group to watch every opening in the deck or turret to smoke the enemy out.[55]

One of the most successful boarding actions occurred on the morning of 22 August 1863 when the USS *Satellite* and *Reliance* were captured as they lay at anchor. Sixty Confederate sailors led by Lieutenant J. Taylor Wood boarded them. Rudolph Sommers, the acting ensign, seized his cutlass and pistol and ran out on deck, but before he could reach the action, the boarders shot him in the neck and, using their swords, overpowered him and locked him in his cabin.[56]

The Confederate Navy was by no means the only side to contemplate the advantages of boarding. In November 1862, Commander J.W.A. Nicholson wrote the commander of the New York Naval Yard suggesting that:

> *In view of the close proximity of the pirate 290 [CSS* Alabama*] to our coast, I would suggest that one of our ocean steamers be chartered .... I would then run alongside of her and capture her by boarding, and as she carries but 90 men, I am confident that the capture can be easily made.*[57]

For the most part, however, officers of the Union Navy were more concerned with repelling boardings than engaging in them. Officers such as J.A.

Dahlgren, Rear-Admiral of the South Atlantic Blockading Squadron, sent numerous letters stressing the vigilance that his captains needed to maintain against the threat of Confederate boarders. In 1864, as the *T. A. Ward* prepared to sail to Calibogue Sound, Dalhgren sent orders to Lieutenant Kennison. In them, he stated, 'in all cases be on your guard against boarders, the small arms stacked conveniently on deck and loaded with buckshot or slugs. The watch on deck should have bowie knives in their belts'.[58] To Commander Colvocoresses onboard the USS *Saratoga* he wrote, 'you are enjoined to pay the strictest attention to security against torpedoes or assault by boarders'.[59]

David D. Porter, Rear-Admiral of the Mississippi Squadron, voiced similar sentiments in 1861: 'The guns must always be kept loaded with grape or canister, and the small arms at hand loaded and ready to repel boarders [60] ... Drill your men twice a day until they are perfectly acquainted with the management of guns and the manner of repelling boarders ....[61] keep everything ready to repel boarders.' Later that year, Foxhall A. Parker, commander of the USS *Release* wrote to Washington regarding his concerns about boarders. He argued that it would be impossible to protect his ship with no netting and his men not properly trained.[62]

The technological advancements of the nineteenth century allowed vessels to repel boarders in new ways that were rapidly rendering axes and pikes obsolete. Using the boiling water from a steam engine was the most popular of these new methods. The *Tennessee* had attachments on the boilers to hold water so the men could throw one stream from forward of the casemate and one aft. When sailors from the *Tyler* and *Carondelet* tried to board the USS *Richmond*, they were repelled with boiling water, and lost a great many men in the process.[63]

In April 1862 Lieutenant Badger of the USS

Anacostia wrote to Lieutenant Wise concerning the possibility that Confederate sailors would try to board the ironclad *Merrimack*, and how they might prevent it:

> It has occurred to me, from the movements of the Merrimack *on her last visit to Hampton Roads, and from other reasons, that the enemy has some plan to draw the* Monitor *out from under the guns of the fortress, in order to capture her by boarding. Suppose half a dozen men were to spring on the* Monitor's *decks provided with grapnels and chains, and make them fast, just after her two guns had been fired; undoubtedly she could be towed off and they could not help themselves. It seems to me that it would not be difficult for them to provide a few men with armor to perform this duty, and with comparative safety, since only musketry could be used against them. In such an event it strikes me that the 'liquid fire,' with which you witnessed an experiment four or five months ago at the navy yard, Washington, would be a good thing to drive them off with. The pipe of a hose thrown out of the small holes in the 'dome,' or out of the pilot house, would, I think, clear the decks sooner than the heaviest discharge of musketry that could possibly be brought to bear. If you think well of this idea, pray call Fox's attention to it. He was present and witnessed the effect of the 'liquid fire' on the occasion referred to.*[64]

Clash of the Ironclads: USS *Monitor* versus CSS *Merrimack*. (Naval Historical Center)

Axes

Axes used by the Royal and US navies from 1840 to 1865 changed dramatically from those used in the past century, as their function onboard ships shifted from weapon/utilitarian object to a strictly utilitarian tool. No longer rounded, manufacturers shortened the blade to have a more squared appearance, and shortened the spike head to half the length of previous models. Although naval axes now appeared more like tomahawks, two grooves were still cut out of the blade to form teeth in American versions. Those used by the Royal Navy kept the down-curving flat spike. The head was attached to the handle through langets secured with two rivets. To help prevent loss, a slot drilled through the bottom of the handle allowed the user to wrap a leather thong around their wrist. Each axe had a leather sheath in order to protect the blade, which was sometime marked with the British broad arrow or 'U.S. Navy'.

Between 1852 and 1866, the US government ordered, issued or stored 5129 axes on board its ships or at the various naval yards. The Ames Manufacturing Company out of Massachusetts and the Underhill Edge Tool Company produced most naval axes. In 1852 the Navy Department entered into a contract with Ames for 300 axes for the naval yards in Boston, Norfolk, and New York at a cost of $1.12 each. As in earlier decades, the only marks on the axe blade were 'AMES' and/or 'US NAVY'. Most ships averaged between 20 and 30 axes.

Axes used by the Confederate Navy were the same style as those used in the North. They acquired them by confiscation from northern ships or produced in factories in the South. Stores were also captured from US naval yards. The largest and best-equipped yard in the US was the Gosport Navy Yard in Norfolk, Virginia. Following Virginia's secession from the Union in 1861, the yard was abandoned and partially destroyed. An immense quantity of

Naval axe from the 1860s listed in Francis Bannerman's catalogue of 1927. (Author's collection)

ordnance was captured by the Confederacy, however, including 141 battle-axes. The Confederacy sometimes purchased axes from abroad, as in 1862, when Raphael Semmes, commander of the CSS *Sumter*, requested, 'axes such as worn by the British seamen' from the Hon. W. L. Yancey, C. S. commissioner, in London.[65]

Pikes

Pikes did not have the utilitarian value of axes, nor offer the personal protection of swords. Although the Royal Navy used the leaf and three-sided blade pike patterns simultaneously in the earlier part of the nineteenth century, by the 1840s it used the three-sided almost exclusively. It contained iron straps that fastened to a hard wood pole. The US Navy ordered and issued more pikes than axes, although there are few cases of boarders actually using them during the war. As with previous models, the type used by both the Union and Confederate navies had either a diamond-shaped or a flat leaf-shaped blade averaging 8in (20.3cm) in length. Blades were marked with the initials 'U.S.', the initials of the inspector, or the naval yard. Shafts were about 11ft (3.4m) long with a rounded butt.

Cutlasses

Between 1840 and 1865 the cutlass of the enlisted man changed dramatically. Up to the 1840s, while of the same general form, a cutlass could vary greatly depending on the manufacturer. In 1840 the Royal Navy addressed growing concern that the guard of the M1814 cutlass did not provide sufficient protection to the user's hand. Therefore, in November 1841 the navy ordered 10,000 new cutlasses at a cost of 4/3d each.[66] The overall design seems to have been modelled after the M1822 heavy cavalry sword, with a slightly curved blade averaging 29½in to 33½in (75 to 85cm) in length terminating in a double-edged spear point. The guard was large, in a basket hilt shape. The Royal Navy used this style until the Second World War.

After more then 20 years without any significant government contracts, the weapon industry in England suffered a severe decline, especially in locations such as Shotley Bridge and Birmingham. Consequently, the government found it difficult to procure the required 10,000 swords. One alternative examined in 1844 was to alter existing stores of swords, both naval and cavalry, for use at sea. This was not a good decision as the weapons proved too brittle for use in combat.

Besides individual contractors, the Royal Small Arms Factory at Enfield produced weapons for the Navy. The Enfield cutlass consisted of a black steel, half-basket guard. The cast iron grip was produced from a mould. The flat blade was slightly curved with a double-edged spear point. The obverse of the blade was engraved with an arrow above the inspector's initials, a crown. The reverse side of the blade was engraved with a production number.

After 1859 Enfield also produced the Enfield Rifle Pattern Cutlass Bayonet. As with other cutlass models, the cutlass-bayonet consisted of a steel half-basket guard with a flat steel blade. The blade differed, however in that it was straight and single-edged. Another difference was in the grip, which was manufactured from two pieces of leather riveted to each side of the tang. The knuckle bow was attached to the pommel with a single rivet and contained a half-inch slot. As with officer swords of this period, the hilt was decorated with a downward curved quillon. The cup-guard terminated in a one-inch circular slot used to fit the sword to the two-band Enfield muskets and the P1861 Enfield Musketoons.

The Royal Navy also imported cutlasses. In 1858, when Charles Reeves & Company out of Birmingham could not complete an order for 15,000 sword bayonets to the navy's satisfaction, they turned to the cutlers in Solingen to produce the needed weapons. By the 1860s the Royal Navy had 78,000 cutlasses at sea and in storage.

Cutlasses in the Royal Navy between 1841 and 1865 were marked with a variety of identification marks including the royal cipher of William IV

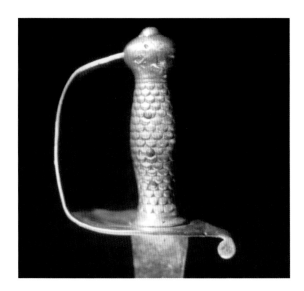

Model 1841 cutlass. (Annapolis Naval Academy Collection)

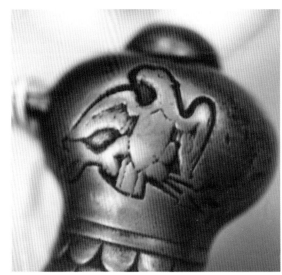

Federal eagle stamped on the hilt of the Model 1841 cutlass. (Annapolis Naval Academy Collection)

BOARDING CUTLASSES ORDERED BY THE ROYAL NAVY, 1845–64[67]

Manufacturer	Number Ordered	Cost (shillings/pence)	Type	Date
Royal Small Arms Factory	15,000	5/0½	Cutlass	1845
John Harvey	4800	4/6	Cutlass	1847
John Heighington	32,620	4/6	Cutlass	1847
Robert Mole	7416	4/6	Cutlass	1847
James Boydell	3600	3/6	Blades	1847
R. & W. Aston	4000	7/-	Cutlass	1859
Chavasse & Company	3000	7/-	Cutlass	1859
C. Reeves	2000	7/-	Cutlass	1859
R. Mole & Son	3000	7/-	Cutlass	1859
G. Robinson	1000	5/6	Cutlass	1859
G. Salter & Son	1000	7/-	Cutlass	1859
T. Lawrence	1000	6/3	Cutlass	1860
Robinson & Watts	2000	6/3	Cutlass	1860
Schnitzler & Kirschbaum	26,732	13/6	Cutlass Bayonet	1859
Weyersberg Brothers	30,000	13/6	Cutlass Bayonet	1859
Höller	13,000	13/6	Cutlass Bayonet	1859
Clauberg	4000	13/6	Cutlass Bayonet	1859
Klönne	1000	13/6	Cutlass Bayonet	1859
C. Reeves	768	13/6	Cutlass Bayonet	1859
Chavasse & Company	1700	13/10	Cutlass Bayonet	1860
T. Moxham	430	13/10	Cutlass Bayonet	1863
C. P. Swinburn & Son	370	13/10	Cutlass Bayonet	1863
R. & W. Aston	900	14/6	Cutlass Bayonet	1864
Total	**158,436**			

(1830–7) and Victoria (1837–1901), a crown over a figure, or a broad arrow. Blades were also stamped with numbers indicating the production sequence or an inspector's mark.

As in the Royal Navy, during the 1840s the US Navy made significant alterations to the weapons carried by enlisted men. In February 1841 the US Navy Department authorised the Ames Manufacturing Company to produce the first standardised cutlass model for use by the US Navy. The sword was the same style as the M1832 foot artillery sword and probably poured from the same mould. The blade, no longer curved and single-edged, was straight, double-edged, and about half the size, averaging 21in (53cm). The hilt was made of sheet brass, and the grip had a moulded design to emulate eagle feathers. Unlike the M1832, manufacturers added a knucklebow to provide protection for the user's hand. The only decoration was a Federal eagle engraved on the pommel. Between 1841 and 1845 the

BOARDING AXES, PIKES, AND SWORDS ISSUED IN THE UNION NAVY 1854–65

Vessel	Axes	Pikes	Swords	Date
Powhatan	0	0	12	Mar 1854
San Jacinto	0	100	100	1851–5
Levant	22	0	22	1851–5
Jamestown	0	0	93	1851–5
John Adams	27	0	0	1851–5
Macedonian	0	10	25	Oct 1855
Preble	3	0	70	May 1857
Merrimack	22	0	0	Sep 1857
Pawnee	5	40	50	Mar 1860
Wabash	4	4	178	Apr 1861
Roanoke	0	0	170	Apr 1861
Savannah	0	0	125	Apr 1861
Potomac	0	0	170	Apr 1861
Quaker City	1	4	350	Early 1861
Dawn	0	0	30	Jun 1861
Samuel Rotan	0	8	16	1862
Commodore Perry	0	10	60	Mar 1862
Somerset	0	0	50	Mar 1862
Marmora	0	20	20	Nov 1862
Indianola	0	0	100	Sep 1862
Paul Jones	0	45	60	Jun 1862
Stepping Stone	0	0	12	Sep 1862
Osage	0	0	50	Feb 1863
Neosho	0	0	50	Feb 1863
Ozark	0	0	20	Feb 1863
Fawn	0	0	40	Feb 1863
Cyane	32	50	173	1863
Saranac	10	48	127	1863
Nansemond	20	0	70	Aug 1863
Primrose	0	10	8	Feb 1863
Tecumseh	24	20	30	Apr 1864
Onondaga	15	0	45	1864
Nereus	30	40	64	1864
Cornubia	0	0	40	1864
Proteus	30	40	64	1864
Hydrangea	6	15	25	1864
Agawan	30	45	70	1864
Canonicus	0	8	50	1864
Massasoit	0	0	90	1864
Opontoosuc	0	0	20	1864
Mattabessett	20	35	50	1864
Picket Boats # 1–6	0	0	7	1864
Oriole	0	20	40	Mar 1865
Colossus	0	20	40	Mar 1865
Gamage	0	0	40	Mar 1865
Banshee	0	0	20	Feb 1865
Total	**301**	**642**	**3021**	

Model 1860 cutlass.
(Annapolis Naval
Academy Collection)

Union Navy ordered 6600 of these cutlasses,[68] and was the model most frequently issued to Confederate vessels during the Civil War. Union-made weapons were often stolen or confiscated from Union ships or were retained by individuals when they resigned from the US Navy. The Confederacy also used older weapons and many vessels were outfitted with cutlasses manufactured by Nathan Starr almost 50 years earlier.

The M1841 proved to be heavy and awkward. Therefore, in 1861, the Navy Department replaced it with a more practical weapon modelled after those used in the French navy. On 18 May 1861 the Navy Department contacted James T. Ames to discuss the specifications of the M1861:

Sir, The Bureau takes this opportunity of informing you that instructions have been issued to Commander Hitchcock to have swords made for the Navy. Enclosed you will find the drawing of a French sword from which the Bureau request you will have a specimen sword of approved steel made and forwarded with all practicable dispatch to this office. The scabbard to be riveted and not sewn, and brass mountings are not required except for the button to confirm the belt.[69]

The blade was single-edged and slightly curved, with one fuller. The brass hilt had a Phrygian helmet pommel and half-basket guard. The grip was leather-covered wood secured with 18 twists of brass wire. The scabbard was made of black leather and secured by a row of brass rivets. Ames marked each cutlass on the guard and upper part of the scabbard with numbers up to 1000 and roman numerals afterwards.[70] Between 1861 and 1864 Ames produced 22,000 of these swords.[71]

* * *

The nineteenth century, with its rapid advancements

in naval technology, rendered many edged weapons ineffective. Axes reverted to utilitarian objects used to fight fires, while firearms, bayonets and other, newer, means of repelling boarders replaced pikes. Only swords advanced and changed as weapons during this period, with the first standardised cutlasses for the enlisted men introduced. Influence for the M1860 came not from the British as in previous decades, but rather from the French navy and other branches within the US military. Furthermore, the Industrial Revolution made it possible for weapons to be mass-produced using moulds, creating a higher production rate then ever before. By the end of the century, however, the use of firearms had eclipsed swords, although they remained popular as dress or presentation pieces.

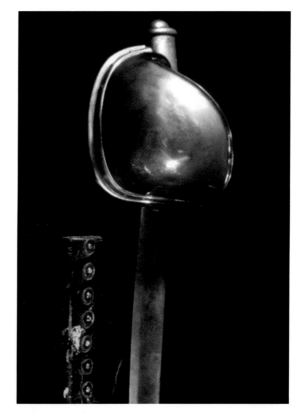

Model 1860 cutlass
hilt. (Annapolis Naval
Academy Collection)

CHAPTER 3

Officer Swords, 1793–1865

During the period 1793–1860 the Royal and United States navies retained a core of young officers different in several respects from those who fought up to and through the Revolutionary War. This diversity can be seen in their organisation, actions and even weapons. Officers carried swords and daggers not only for personal protection but also in order to reflect their wealth, rank, social status and political or religious affiliations. Officers chose their weapons carefully because of these connotations, and consequently there were almost as many different types as there were officers. Even after regulation weapons were issued, officers still modified the design or the quality of the materials to distinguish their weapon from those of other officers.

This chapter will survey the background of the officers that made up the Royal and US Navies and the popular style of swords and/or daggers they carried. Most officers owned at least two swords. The first was his fighting weapon, used in battle and only plainly decorated. The second was his dress sword, lavishly decorated, as its primary purpose was to

Admiral Duncan receiving the sword of the defeated Dutch Admiral de Winter after the Battle of Camperdown, 11 October 1797. (National Maritime Museum)

show rank and status. However, this is not always a hard and fast rule, as there are in existence examples of lavishly-decorated fighting swords and simple, unadorned dress swords. Finally, a sovereign, the government, a group of peers or private organisations such as the Lloyd's Patriotic Fund, might award an officer a presentation sword for bravery in battle.

Officer swords 1793–1849

For the purposes of this book, an officer is defined as any man who held his position by either commission or warrant. In the Royal Navy the Board of Admiralty appointed commissions to admirals, vice-admirals, rear-admirals, commodores, captains, commanders, and lieutenants.[1] Other officers – such as masters, surgeons, pursers, chaplains, boatswains, carpenters, and gunners – held their rank through warrants issued by the Navy Board.[2]

Unlike the cutbacks faced by the enlisted men in the years after the Napoleonic Wars, the number of officers commissioned in the Royal Navy actually increased during by 48 per cent during this period, from 2949 in 1799 to 5664 in 1820. Every officer who was not employed during this time was still maintained on half-pay.

NUMBER OF OFFICERS IN THE ROYAL NAVY, 1799–1812

Rank	1799	1812
Flag Officers		
Admirals	41	62
Vice-Admirals	42	65
Rear-Admirals	49	60
Post Captains	495	777
Commanders	319	586
Lieutenants	2003	3104
Total	**2949**	**4654**

SOCIAL BACKGROUND OF ROYAL NAVY OFFICERS, 1793–1815[4]

Background	Percentage
Gentry	27.4
Navy	24.1
Others	11.0
Titled (Peers/Baronets)	12.0
Church	8.7
Army	7.3
Public Office	5.7
Medicine	2.8
Members of Parliament	1.0

During the eighteenth century young boys with officer aspirations entered the navy between the ages of 11 and 13 as a captain's servant, or might be rated as an ordinary or able seaman. Captains were allowed four boys per hundred crewmen, but by 1793 this arrangement had been abolished in favour of a volunteer system.[3] Once designated an able seaman, the next step was midshipman. They then spent at least three years training at sea, some being promoted to master's mate. Most midshipmen learned their craft onboard the ship they served, but some trained at the Royal Naval College in Portsmouth (before it was closed in the 1830s). With a minimum of six years of sea service, three of which had to be as a midshipman, the 'young gentlemen' were then eligible to take the lieutenant's examination. Thereafter, promotion to commander and post captain depended on circumstance: it might be gained by meritorious service, or by that subtle machinery of family and political influence known as 'interest', or most commonly by a combination of both. Advancement from Post Captain to flag rank, however, was governed by strict seniority, although in wartime very talented officers could be elevated by retiring their seniors as 'yellow admirals'. Needless to say, in the peacetime years after 1815 such promotion was the exception rather than the rule.

Promotion was only one part of career advancement, because there was also the question of an appointment. Even in wartime, it was an achievement to remain continuously employed, and after 1815 it was common for every appointment to have at least 50 officers competing for it. Those without political or family connections could wait their entire career between appointments.

The young men who entered the Royal Navy during this period came from a wide range of backgrounds. By far the largest social groups included the gentry and families with a long tradition of naval service.[5] Other officers were the children of professional men such as doctors and lawyers, some were from the aristocracy, while others had family ties to the state, church or army. The social background of these men did not change dramatically throughout the century, and the beliefs and values they carried can be seen in the decorations used to adorn the weapons they chose to carry.

The period from 1793 to 1815 is considered by most historians to be the golden age of the Royal Navy, in which such iconic figures as Thomas Cochrane, Cuthbert Collingwood, Richard Howe, Edward Pellew and William Sidney Smith helped project Britain's power on the high seas. Honour, service and valour were important attributes to these men and no officer enshrined this attitude more clearly than Horatio, Lord Nelson. In 1897 noted maritime historian, Alfred Thayer Mahan described Nelson as 'the one man who in himself summed up and embodied the greatness of the possibilities which Sea Power comprehends ... the man for whom genius and opportunity worked together, to make him the personification of the Navy of Great Britain.'[6]

Born on 29 September 1758, Nelson was only 12 when appointed a midshipman aboard his uncle's ship HMS *Raisonnable*. A year later he sailed to the West Indies aboard a merchantman. This was not unusual however, as most officers spent their time in between naval assignments gaining experience on merchantmen. In 1776, Nelson fell ill while sailing back to England aboard HMS *Dolphin*. During this time he had a spiritual experience that convinced him one day he would become a hero in the service of his king and country. Seven years after joining the navy, Nelson was promoted to Lieutenant on HMS *Lowestoffe*. After this Nelson quickly moved up the ranks to Commander by 20, Post Captain the following year, Commodore by 38, and Vice-Admiral by 43.

At the outbreak of the war with Napoleon in 1793, Nelson was commanding officer of HMS *Agamemnon*, sailing with Lord Hood's Mediterranean Fleet and assisting in the blockade of Toulon and later in the capture of the Corsican ports of Bastia and Calvi. It was during this time that he distinguished himself as and innovative and daring commander. In 1796 after promoted to commodore, Nelson was transferred to HMS *Captain*. A year later in February 1797, his capture of the Spanish *San Nicolas* (80 guns) and *San Josef* (112 guns) at the Battle of Cape St Vincent was followed by promotion to the rank of rear-admiral and the gift of several presentation swords.

On 1 August 1798 Nelson was once again victorious over the French at the Battle of the Nile (also known as the Battle of Aboukir Bay). As a result, Napoleon's plan to take the war with Britain to India failed. For his part in the battle, Nelson was granted the title of Baron and awarded numerous presentation swords by organisations such as the Patriotic Fund and Egyptian Club. In 1801 he further distinguished himself through his actions at the Battle of Copenhagen. During this hard-fought encounter he famously disregarded the signal to withdraw and continued the battle until achieving an important strategic victory for Britain. During the Battle of Trafalgar on 21 October 1805 he employed aggressive tactics against a joint fleet of French and Spanish vessels. Although he won the battle, he was mortally wounded by a French sniper and died several hours later. The confrontation demonstrated Nelson's belief in the superiority of not only the Royal Navy's tactics but also the fighting capabilities of its men in close combat at sea: although attempts were made, during this battle no British ship was successfully boarded.

Gallantry, initiative, and originality were main

factors in Nelson's career, although honour and duty were just as important. In a letter to his future wife Frances Nisbet he wrote, 'Duty is the greatest business of a Sea Officer. All private considerations must give way to it, however Painful it is.' Before the Battle of Trafalgar he signalled his fleet from HMS *Victory*, the now famous saying, 'England expects that every man will do his duty.' Nelson was not the only officer during this period to believe these sentiments, and the faith and confidence that he placed in every man having a sense of honour and duty was certainly warranted.

While the officers of the Royal Navy had a rich heritage dating back centuries, the United States Navy was still very young and inexperienced. After the Revolutionary War, the Continental Navy sold all of its vessels, as there was neither the need nor the budget for a standing navy. After the war, the US Congress handled the regulation and maintenance of both the navy and the army,[7] but in 1789 created the

Stephen Decatur Jr. (Naval Historical Center)

Benjamin Stoddert, Secretary of the Navy, 1798–1801. (Naval Historical Center)

War Department to perform these tasks. In the years that followed, American shipping faced numerous threats from the Barbary Powers (Algeria, Tripoli, Tunis, and Morocco) and later by the French in the Quasi War that forced the War Department to expand the size and role of the navy.

On 27 March 1794 Congress passed an act establishing the first naval force under the US Constitution.[8] This action called for the construction or purchase of six vessels, four of 44 guns and two of 36 guns. It was also the first to establish officer numbers, ranks and describe pay and rations in detail, although it did not regulate the weapons officers should carry.[9] The newly-established system of rank closely resembled that used by the British.[10] The Senate nominated and confirmed all commissioned officers, including captains, masters, commandants, lieutenants, surgeons, surgeon's

Sword presented by Congress to Captain Stephen Decatur Jr. in 1804. (Annapolis Naval Academy Collection)

mates and pursers. Other officers – such as midshipmen, sailing masters and chaplains – held their positions by warrants issued by the President and the Secretary of the Navy, but not approved by the Senate.[11] Unlike the Royal Navy, the highest level of promotion was to captain, not admiral, and surgeons, surgeon's mates, and pursers held commissions not warrants.

OFFICERS IN THE AMERICAN NAVY, 1801–12

Rank	1801	1806	1812
Captain	28	13	12
Master Commandants	7	9	10
Lieutenants	110	72	73
Midshipmen	354	150	310
Marine Officers	—	—	42
Total	**499**	**244**	**447**

After Congress established the Navy Department in 1798, Benjamin Stoddert was appointed the first Secretary. He held this post until 1801.[12] In 1799, one of the first modifications he made was to change the organisation and pay for officers. First, the number of officers appointed to a ship depended upon the vessel's size. Second, the Navy Department created a new rank with the addition of master commandant, which ranked below a captain but ahead of a lieutenant.

Between the years 1775 and 1815, there was a dramatic change in the views and backgrounds of the officers who made up the US Navy. In 1797 officers who commanded American warship – such as John Barry, Thomas Truxtun, Silas Talbot and Stephen Decatur Sr. – had all fought in the Revolutionary War, and before that been British or French citizens. Therefore, their attitudes towards Britain and the United States differed from the views of the younger generation. Christopher McKee, the

OFFICERS PER VESSEL IN THE AMERICAN NAVY, 1812

44 Guns	36 Guns	Sloop
Captain	Captain	Captain
5 lieutenants	5 lieutenants	2 lieutenants
Chaplain	Chaplain	Chaplain
Surgeon	Surgeon	Surgeon
2 surgeon's mates	2 surgeon's mates	1 surgeon's mate
16 midshipmen	12 midshipmen	4–6 midshipmen

historian of the US Navy officer corps, argues that the early American government modelled the structure and organisation of their new navy after the Royal Navy, and this fact influenced the character and views of those first officers.[13] British citizens were often allowed to enlist in the navy, and their presence helped to foster this cross-cultural exchange. Most American officers wanted to emulate the Royal Navy and frequently read professional British naval publications such as the *Naval Chronicle*. Lieutenant Cyrus Talbot, after losing the rudder of his brig *Richmond* in a gale in 1799, turned to the British book *A System of Naval Tactics, Combining the Established Theory with General Practice, and Particularly with the Present Practice of the British Navy* for an answer to his dilemma.[14] Not all officers embraced this emulation of British ways. Thomas Truxtun distrusted the enlistment of British citizens into the American Navy, and warned the Secretary of War in 1797, 'to introduce foreigners into our navy would appear to me a very dangerous policy.'[15]

Around 1800, there was a shift in the views of the officer corps as younger officers moved up the ranks to command vessels. These younger officers did not remember the Revolutionary War, and had never been British citizens. An example of this shift in views and backgrounds can be seen in the careers of Stephen Decatur, Sr., and his son Stephen Jr. Before 1794, many US sailors began their maritime profession not in the navy but rather on merchant vessels, and Stephen Decatur Sr. was no exception. French by birth, he emigrated to America, and went to sea at an early age. In 1774, at the age of 22, he became master of the merchant vessel *Peggy*, and made a fortune attacking British commerce as a privateer during the Revolutionary War. After the war, Decatur returned to the merchant service until 1798, when he took command of the 20-gun *Delaware* in the Quasi-War with France.

Unlike his father, Stephen Decatur Jr. did not remember being a foreign subject. Born in 1779, he was only four when the Revolutionary War ended. His naval career began in 1798 when he became a midshipman aboard the frigate *United States* commanded by Captain John Barry. Decatur rose quickly through the ranks; only a year after joining the navy, Congress promoted him to the rank of lieutenant. During the Barbary Wars, he led a daring raid into the harbour of Tripoli that destroyed the US frigate *Philadelphia*, which had been captured by the Tripolitans after running aground. This action earned him a promotion to the rank of captain and a presentation sword, voted to him by the members of Congress.

At the outbreak of the War of 1812, Decatur was commanding officer of the frigate *United States*. As master of that ship, he defeated and captured the British frigate *Macedonian* in October 1812. The next year, Congress promoted him to the rank of commodore. In January 1815, while in command of the frigate *President*, he encountered the British blockading squadron off New York. He fought off the *Endymion* but with his ship disabled, he was forced to surrender to the rest of the British squadron.

Aside from the bravery and ingenuity shown in Decatur's career, honour was important to him, and he was not afraid to defend it through duelling. He was not unique in this respect. In the early part of

the nineteenth century 18 officers died while participating in duels (12 midshipmen, four lieutenants, a surgeon, and a surgeon's mate).[16] Duels usually occurred over a minor incident, where sailors exchanged harsh words, and sometimes physical blows that could not be resolved with an apology. This then put the challenger and the challenged in a precarious situation: if either one refused to fight, the crew would label him a coward and ostracise him.

In 1799 Decatur fought his first duel with the encouragement of his father. At that time, he was the lieutenant of the *United States*, and the commander sent him to Philadelphia to recruit men. While there, some enlisted men fled to an Indiaman. When he went to retrieve them, the chief mate adamantly refused, insulting both Decatur and the American Navy. Decatur maintained his temper and left the ship. His father, upon hearing of the incident, insisted that his son challenge the man to a duel, not only to defend his honour, but also to defend the honour of the navy.[17] During the duel, Decatur realised that the man was not experienced with firearms, and only injured him, thereby proving both his courage and his chivalry.

Lieutenants were not the only officers to participate in duels as lower officers and midshipmen were more prone to participate in this activity. Midshipmen William L. Rodgers and A. Philips, both of the USS *Constellation*, nearly came to blows in 1813 over a trivial dispute when Phillips accidentally placed Rodgers' laundry on a greasy table. A few days after the argument, Rodgers formally issued a challenge to Philips by posting a note at the local tavern in Norfolk, Virginia:

I regret extremely My Necessity to reduce to infamy Any Man, but a duty which honor imposes, & Justice Sanctions, compels me to give publicity to the following Notice. Mr. Philips Midshipman on board the U.S. Frigate

Constellation *having publicly Charged Me as devoid of truth & honor, neither of which Charges he has Ability to prove just, & having refused to render Me, the satisfaction I had a right to demand & expect have No other Alternative but to publish him to the world as A Liar & a Coward. His having ungenerously held me up to public view without Advertising Me of his intention, discovers a heart, devoid of every principle which Constitutes the Gentleman Man of honour.*[18]

Rodgers was dismissed from the navy before the duel could take place but after issuing an apology was allowed to return. Officers such as captains, masters, master commandants and sailing masters are not recorded as having ever participated in duelling. Most were older and did not feel a need to maintain or increase their status or self-esteem by resorting to a duel. Throughout the later part of the eighteenth century up to 1815, only 1 per cent of officers died in a duel, the most famous being the duel between Stephen Decatur Jr. and James Barron in 1820, in which Decatur was killed.[19]

The sword that an officer carried was as important as the values of honour and courage that he held. When an enemy captured a vessel, the officers' swords were taken as a token of their surrender. After Commodore Horatio Nelson captured the *San Josef* and *San Nicolas* at the Battle of Cape St Vincent, he was presented with the sword of the vanquished Spanish captain:

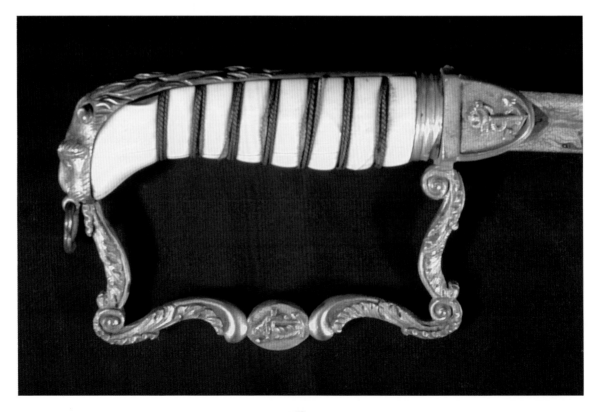

Lion-head pommel sword. (Annapolis Naval Academy Collection)

When I [Nelson] got into her main-chains, a Spanish Officer came upon the quarter-deck rail, without arms, and said the Ship had surrendered. From this welcome information, it was not long before I was on the quarter-deck, when the Spanish Captain, with a bended knee, presented me his Sword, and told me the Admiral was dying with his wounds below. I gave him my hand, and desired him to call to his Officers and Ship's Company that the Ship had surrendered, which he did; and on the quarter-deck of a Spanish First-rate, extravagant as the story may seem, did I receive the Swords of the vanquished Spaniards, which as I received I gave to William Fearney, one of my bargemen, who placed them, with the greatest sang-froid, under his arm.[20]

Slotted-hilt sword. (National Maritime Museum)

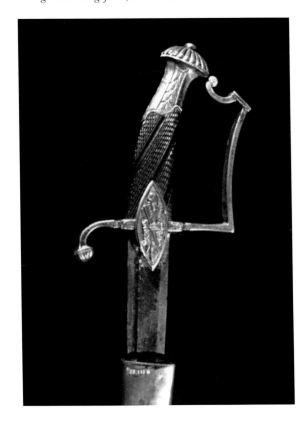

French-influenced hilt used by American naval officers. (Annapolis Naval Academy Collection)

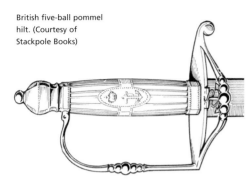

British five-ball pommel hilt. (Courtesy of Stackpole Books)

Later that year, on 11 October 1797, Admiral Duncan received the sword of the Dutch Admiral de Winter after defeating him at the Battle of Camperdown. When Truxtun captured the vessel *L'Insurgente* in 1799 First Lieutenant Bartholomew Clinch recorded that:

> *He [Truxtun] presented the four Navy lieutenants, the Sailing Master & Myself [First Lieutenant Bartholomew Clinch, US Marine Corps] each with a Sword taken from the French Officers [Insurgente] as a token of approbation of our respective Conduct & I protest that given to me was the second best in the whole.*[21]

Captain John Rodgers, who visited Algiers in 1806, recorded another example of the importance an officer placed on his sword, in a letter to the Secretary of the Navy later that year:

> *I am the first Christian that has ever been permitted to visit a Dey of Algiers with Side Arms, and I think it worth remarking to you, particularly as I have Coll reasons to believe, he has understood by Lears Dfrogeman, that a refusal to receive me with my Sword, would be to him a deprivation.*[22]

Fighting Swords

Before the 1790s, neither the Board of Admiralty nor the US government regulated the type of sword an officer could carry. Moreover, most officers purchased their swords outside government channels, which meant they varied far more than the cutlasses issued to enlisted men. On 24 August 1791, however, the US Secretary of War issued the first regulations, not only in an attempt to control the immense variety of officer sword styles, but also to provide a distinctive form of rank identification.[23] The regulations were very broad though, specifying only 'yellow mounted cut and thrust weapons'.[24] It was a start, and a formal type of rank identification was preferred in the US Navy as it grew in size and power.[25] It would be another 14 years before the Royal Navy issued any regulations regarding officer swords.

Swords played a significant role in early rank identification. Officers could determine a person's status and specialisation by his sword's decoration, blade design, or hilt design. The hilt of a commander would have a white ivory grip, whereas lieutenants, masters, mates and midshipmen had black grips.[26] Preference was not the only determining factor in the type of sword an officer chose to carry; financial resources also came into play. Officers with modest incomes bought cheaper swords, while those with more money could afford

Five-ball pommel fragments recovered from the wreck of HM Brig *DeBraak*. (Delaware State Museum)

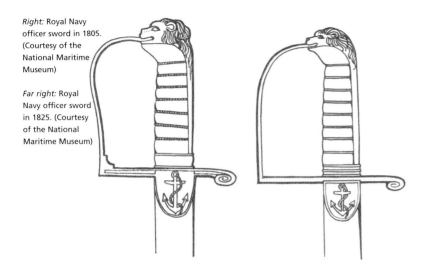

lavishly decorated weapons. Frequently, they bought these blades from London cutlers who imported weapons from the famous swordsmiths of Solingen, Germany, or Klingenthal, France. These weapons were not only prestigious, but spoke of their wealth and status. Officers also looked overseas to obtain their weapons because of the difficulty in acquiring good domestic weapons. This was not because local cutlers were not capable; by the early nineteenth century, England and America had respected sword-making industries with the likes of the Birmingham cutlers in England and Nathan Starr Sr. and William Rose in America. The problem was that these contractors normally spent their time engaged with government contracts, and had little time to fill orders for individual officers.

Up to the nineteenth century, fighting swords carried by officers of both the Royal and American navies closely resembled those used at the same time by the army. During the first 30 years of the eighteenth century, hunting swords were the most commonly carried version, but by the 1750s were replaced with other styles, such as the smallsword and hanger. Similar to the infantry hanger, those used by naval officers had a slightly curved, double-edged blade, 28 to 32in (71 to 81cm) in length, with a round pommel and simple guard. Hangers and hunting swords were popular among naval officers because their size made them easier to use in the confined space aboard ship. After 1789, American naval officers began to adopt models used by the French.[27] French models were lighter with a single large shell on the obverse of the hilt, which turned toward the point, and adorned with nautical emblems.[28]

Although there was very little variation in blade design during the early 1800s, three dominant hilt styles were carried by British and American naval officers. The first was the slotted hilt hanger used by officers in both navies since the American Revolution. The hilt contained two slots that ran parallel on the guard and knucklebow, and decorated with fouled anchors.[29] By the 1790s, the earlier fluted olive pommel had been abandoned in favour of other designs influenced by the tastes of individual officers. Some had capstan rivets; others were decorated with lion-head, dog-head or eagle-head pommels. Manufacturers also ribbed the ivory

Eagle-head pommel sword commonly carried by American naval officers in the 1830s. (Annapolis Naval Academy Collection)

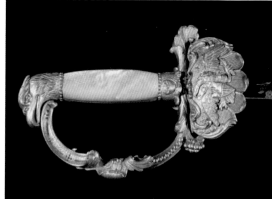

Left: Five-ball guard fragments recovered from the wreck of HM Brig *DeBraak*. (Delaware State Museum)

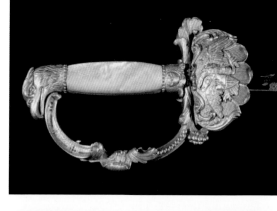

Eagle-head pommel sword commonly carried by American naval officers in the 1830s. (Annapolis Naval Academy Collection)

Below and Below left: Sword worn by Commodore Edward Preble, Commanding US Mediterranean Squadron. (Annapolis Naval Academy Collection)

Variation of the M1827 Officer Sword. It varies in the open work and in place of the royal insignia, a Federal Eagle. (Annapolis Naval Academy Collection)

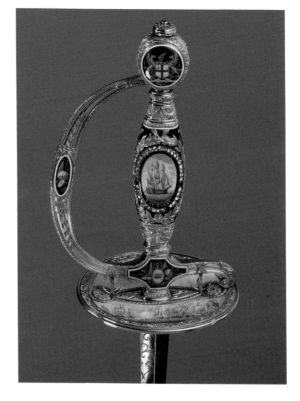

Presentation smallsword. (National Maritime Museum)

Lloyd's Patriotic Fund sword. (National Maritime Museum)

Above: Official regulation drawing of the 1841 Naval Officer Sword. (US National Archives)

Right: Admiral Farragut's 1841 naval fighting sword. (Annapolis Naval Academy Collection)

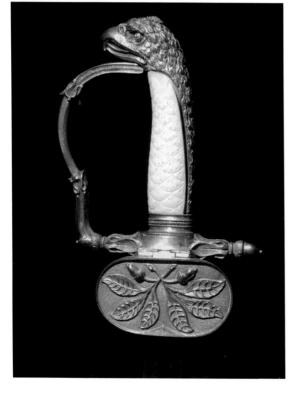

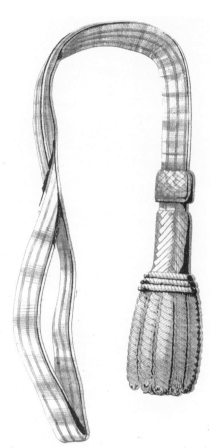

Sword knot. (US National
Archives)

or wooden grip for a better grip.[30]

By 1800 slotted hilt swords had all but disappeared, having been eclipsed by the five-ball hanger. This style had a square-sectioned, reeded ivory grip, an outer guard with five balls, and a series of five balls on the knuckle bow. The British army used this style after 1780 and it was adopted by officers of the Royal Navy in 1790.[31] The only difference between the two variants was the replacement of regimental ciphers on the hilt with a crown over a fouled anchor. In the early nineteenth century, prominent American and British officers carried this type of sword as their fighting weapon. Admiral Duncan carried it as his fighting sword at the Battle of Camperdown in 1797.[32] Captain Philip B.V. Broke, commander of the British frigate *Shannon*, was carrying a five-ball hilted sword when he captured the American frigate *Chesapeake* in 1813. Commodore Edward Preble, commander of US naval forces in the Mediterranean during the Tripolitan War, carried it as his fighting sword,[33] although he replaced the crown and fouled anchor with an eagle atop a liberty bell.

The third hilt style carried between 1790 and 1815 was the stirrup hilt sword. In 1796, the British light cavalry ordered a new sabre,[34] reflecting the need of cavalrymen to have a shorter weapon that was easier to wield. By August 1805, the Navy had copied it, making it their first regulation naval sword. The lion-head pommel, so popular in England during the late eighteenth and early nineteenth

centuries was the only major addition.[35] A fouled anchor replaced regiment ciphers on the langet. This became the basic hilt style for the next 25 years, with changes only to the design of the lion and the shape of the knuckle guard.[36]

In 1825, the Board of Ordnance modified the M1805 by altering the knuckle bow from a reverse 'P' to a reversed 'D' shape. The M1825 carried by lieutenants and above, had a 32in (81cm) grooved blade that manufacturers blued and engraved with nautical and floral motifs. It had a lion-head pommel with ivory grip, and a langet decorated with a fouled anchor. Masters and warrant officers carried the same sword, but with a fish-skin grip, plain pommel and undecorated blade.

In 1827 the Board of Ordnance determined that the revisions introduced in 1825 were not as efficient as they had hoped and discarded the style in favour of a cup-guard pattern. This alteration may have been in response to officer complaints that the modified M1825 did not provide enough protection during combat. The new regulation sword was based on a similar pattern carried by army officers, with a solid half-basket hilt made of brass and opened bars encircling the Royal insignia over a fouled anchor. The only attribute preserved from the M1805 and M1825 was the lion-head pommel.

In 1832 warrant officers such as masters, mates and midshipmen formally adopted a plain version of the M1827 with black fish-skin grip. The lion-head pommel was also replaced with a plain capstan. The difference in decoration and grip colour from those carried by commissioned officers was intended to create an easy means of differentiating between the ranks. Furthermore, it provided lieutenants and above with a more elaborate and prestigious weapon to carry.

In America, naval officers frequently carried the

same styles of weapon as in the Royal Navy, with the addition of some type of distinctive American decoration. Between 1815 and 1840, without any definitive regulations in place, officers carried a wide range of eagle-head pommel swords. The first popular style was based on an infantry pattern and had a brass eagle-head pommel that terminated in a wooden grip covered with mother of pearl. The reverse 'P' knuckle bow was ornately decorated with floral and geometric designs. The semi-circular guard was ornately decorated with relief designs commonly patriotic in nature, including eagles, flags and liberty figures. Another variation of this sword had a small triangular langet decorated with a nautical motif. A second popular style was modelled after the Royal Navy's M1827. It had a brass eagle-head pommel instead of a lion head, a folding counterguard and a sharkskin grip. The guard was an open-work cup containing a raised medallion decorated with an eagle sitting atop an anchor surrounded by stars instead of a crown over a fouled anchor. The blade was frequently engraved with 'United States Navy', eagles, a sailor, shield, anchor and arms.

In 1841 a new era in sword design began when the Navy Department issued the first fully-illustrated regulation sword that doubled as both a fighting and a dress sword. It had an eagle-head pommel, with plumage extending the entire length of the back piece, reverse 'P' knuckle-bow, and hinged oval counterguards on both the obverse and reverse sides. Designers decorated the front counterguard with crossing oak leaf branches and acorns. They pierced the knuckle bow for a sword knot, and decorated the forward half with raised floral designs. The quillons are in the form of acorns and decorated with floral designs. Most had bone grips carved into a number of geometric shape, such as intersecting diagonal lines (chequered appearance), or carved to emulate feathers.

The M1841 had a slightly curved, single-edged blade, with a false edge extending back about 8in (20.3cm) from the point. Blade dimensions averaged 36in (91.4cm) in length and were about 1¼in (3.2cm) wide. The obverse and reverse sides of the blade were etched with a fouled anchor a circle of stars and a sprig of oak leaves and acorns. The scabbard was made of black leather with brass mounts. The throat was decorated with a circle of stars surrounded by floral designs, the middle band with a fouled anchor and floral decorations, and the tip with the typical naval sprays of leaves and acorns.

Officers also carried a much shorter edged weapon known as a dirk or dagger. Traditionally associated exclusively with midshipmen, some commissioned and even Flag Officers continued to carry their dirk long after their midshipman days. Some naval officers would use a dirk and sword simultaneously during battles. From the 1770s to 1825 the Board of Ordnance did not issue any regulations regarding the type of dirk an officer should wear, and most tended to carry smaller versions of popular sword styles. In 1795 officers carried a five-ball side-ring dirk similar in design to the five-ball hilt popular at the same time. The blade was straight, double-edged with an elliptical or diamond cross-section. A central groove helped to strengthen the blade. Most blades ranged between 5 and 16in (12.7 and 40.6cm) long. After 1800, most dirks had the lion-head pommel. Other dirks of this period had curved flat-back blades and plain pommels. The grip was manufactured from black ebony and partially diamond knurled. The quillons were straight with inversed ends. The curvature of the blade made this version impractical as a weapon and may have been produced as a presentation piece for acts of heroism in battle.

In the British uniform regulations of 1825,

midshipmen were forbidden from wearing dirks. By 1856, however, this was reversed and midshipmen and naval cadets were no longer allowed to carry a regulation sword but rather were ordered to carry dirks instead. Similar to models carried in the early 1800s, it had a lion-head pommel, white fish skin grip, and a straight double-edged blade. The hilt was decorated with quillons in the shape of acorns and a fouled anchor. The blade was decorated with a crown over a fouled anchor, foliage and geometric designs.

Sword knots were another means of expressing wealth and prestige. In the Royal and American navies, they became popular on fighting swords around the beginning of the eighteenth century.[37] Sword knots were lengths of cord or leather attached to the guard near the pommel. There were no regulations covering sword knots during the period covered in this book. After 1750 they were yellow or blue tinted, sometimes made of silk, and decorated with a fouled anchor sewn on

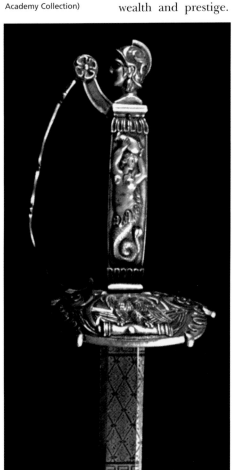

Sword given to Midshipman James Bliss for his involvement in the Battle of Lake Erie, 10 September 1813. (Annapolis Naval Academy Collection)

1812 presentation sword. (Annapolis Naval Academy Collection)

Left and centre: Sword presented by Congress to Captain Stephen Decatur Jr. in 1804. (Annapolis Naval Academy Collection)

Alligator-hilt presentation sword given to captains who fought at the Battle of the Nile, 1 August 1798. (National Maritime Museum)

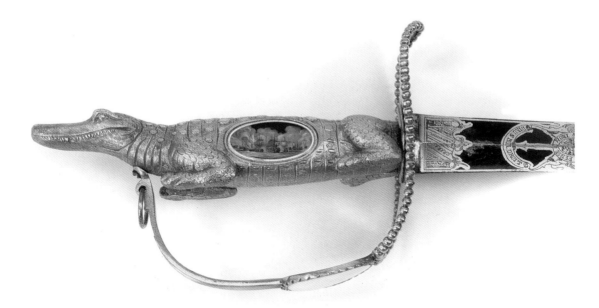

Alligator-hilt presentation sword given to captains who fought at the Battle of the Nile, 1 August 1798. (National Maritime Museum)

the tassel.[38] Officers wrapped the cord around their wrist so that the sword would not be lost in combat and, after 1790, wrapped a length of material around the grip to hide the knuckle bow. Sword knots were also used to decorate civilian and military dress swords.[39]

Dress and presentation swords

Every officer had a fighting sword for battles and a more elaborately decorated dress sword. Officers carried these weapons on social, official and ceremonial occasions.[40] Swords not only conveyed an officer's rank but also his social status. As with fighting swords, dress swords were often patterned after those used by the army. At times, the only distinguishable trait between the two was some type of nautical engraving on the hilt or blade.

By the 1750s, the most popular dress swords carried by British and American officers were smallswords. By 1800, however, eagle-head pommels had replaced them as the most popular weapon in America.[41] Since manufacturers produced hilts one at a time, weapons could vary greatly from one to another and from maker to maker. Cutlers generally used a wooden mould to cast a wax model of the guard and pommel, and then hand-finished it before assembling it to meet the customer's specification.[42]

Hilts also varied depending on the cost of the sword and the materials used such (*eg* gold, ivory or jewels). During the late eighteenth and early nineteenth centuries, grips were often made of ivory or bone. In England, naval officers used the same types of dress swords, with the exception that they preferred lion-head pommels to the eagle-head version so popular in America.

Beginning around 1760, European sovereigns or governments presented individuals with highly ornate swords to commemorate bravery or otherwise distinguished military service.[43] One such organisation was the City of London, which between 1797 and 1846 awarded 25 individuals with presentation swords. By the end of the eighteenth century when the popularity of the small sword declined as a fighting and dress sword, it became fashionable as a presentation piece. These small swords were highly ornate, with hilts made of blue enamel with painted miniatures, jewels, and gilded and blued blades.

In 1803 the Patriotic Fund was established at Lloyd's of London by a group of merchants and underwriters. The swords produced by this group are some of the best-known pieces from England during the nineteenth century, and ushered in a new period for presentation swords in which the small sword was discarded for a new style. The main shape of the sword was the same for all recipients, only the materials and level of embellishment varying. Modelled after the light cavalry sword used by the British Army after 1804, the stirrup hilt contained an ivory grip with a lion-head pommel. The back-piece was decorated to look like the lion's mane. The quillon was formed to look like Roman fasces and

Confederate officers. (Virginia Historical Society)

FLAG OFFICER   CAPTAIN   LIEUTENANT   SURGEON

the guard the club of Hercules with an entwined snake. The triangular langets were decorated with floral designs and a relief design. The blade was blued, slightly curved and decorated with the description of why the sword was presented and gilded designs. The scabbard differed depending on the value of the sword, but was generally as ornately decorated as the sword itself in relief designs and miniature scenes.

Midshipmen, sailors, lieutenants, and Royal Marines were awarded weapons valued at £30 or £50. Between 1803 and 1811 the Fund awarded sixteen £30 swords and ninety-five £50 swords to 76 Lieutenants, 20 Captains, 8 midshipmen, 1 major, and 6 sailors. Sixty-seven £100 swords were awarded to 60 Captains, 2 Commanders, 4 Lieutenants, and 1 Brigadier General. Of the total swords awarded, 14 went to Royal Marines and 4 to army officers.[44]

NUMBER OF SWORDS AWARDED BY THE PATRIOTIC FUND, 1803–11

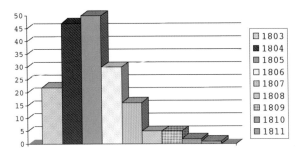

The City of London and the Egyptian Club (for officers involved in the Battle of the Nile) also presented swords to notable officers.[45] The Egyptian Club preferred to create swords that were unique to the specific event for which they presented a sword, including both form and decoration. The sword presented to Lord Nelson for his heroic actions at the Battle of the Nile on 1 August 1798 was a highly ornate weapon with a grip in the shape of an alligator, jewels and miniature scenes of the battle. Cheaper copies were also made and presented to the captains who fought alongside Nelson.

The third type of presentation sword given to officers of the Royal Navy was based upon the regulation sword. Although maintaining the look of the official requirements, the sword was more ornately decorated on the back-piece, knuckle bow, and guard. The blade contained some of the decorations of the regulation sword, but also included accounts of the event that warranted the presentation of a sword.

The American government did not adopt the custom of presenting swords until the 1780s. Furthermore, unlike Britain where presentation swords were at first unique in design and later based on regulation patterns, the United States initially awarded weapons indistinguishable from dress swords and later regulation patterns, but eventually developed weapons completely unique in design.

In 1785 Congress authorised Colonel David Humphreys, Secretary of the American Legislation in Paris, to obtain ten silver-hilted smallswords from French swordsmiths. They then voted to present them to officers who performed commendable actions during the Revolutionary War. Only one naval officer, Commodore John Hazelwood, received one of these weapons, since most of the significant fighting during the war had occurred on land. Around 1800, hangers became popular for recognising distinguished naval action. These weapons were more elaborate then the plain smallswords previously given. Stephen Decatur Jr. received one for the destruction of the US frigate *Philadelphia* after it had fallen into enemy hands.

Originally, both the British and the American government had to look abroad to acquire presentation swords, mainly from Solingen, Germany. By the

Above, above centre and far right: Close-up of the 1841 presentation sword with diamond eye. (Annapolis Naval Academy Collection)

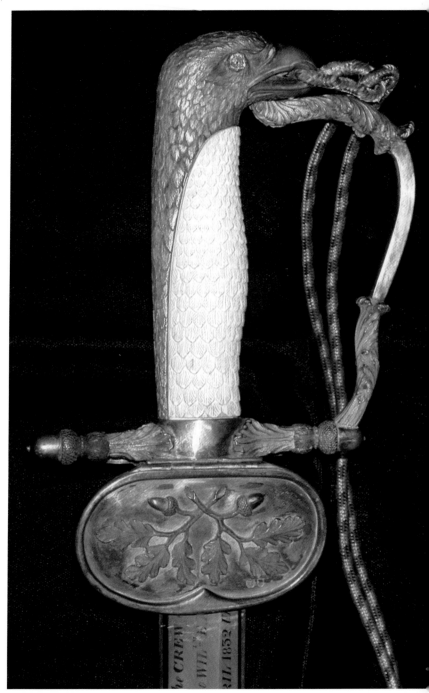

Right: Example of a sword carried by Confederate naval officers. (Annapolis Naval Academy Collection)

Scabbard tip of M1852 US regulation sword. (Virginia Historical Society Collection)

M1861 Naval 'Officer' cutlass. (Annapolis Naval Academy Collection)

Right and above:
Variation of the Model 1852 officer sword used as a dress sword. (Annapolis Naval Academy Collection)

beginning of the nineteenth century, however, the sword industry in both countries had advanced to such a degree that these weapons could be found domestically. The swords produced in the United States by craftsman such as Johnson and Reat of Baltimore, William Rose or Thomas Fletcher of Philadelphia, and Nathan Starr of Connecticut easily rivalled those made abroad.

Officer swords 1850s–65

By the 1850s, the Royal Navy entered a period of reform in an attempt to increase the professionalism of the officer corps. In connection with this, the first formal education facility for the training of naval cadets was introduced. In previous centuries, men entered service at a very young age through some type of interest as 'captain's servants', instead of

Admiral Farragut. (Naval Historical Center)

USS *Governor Moore*. (Naval Historical Center)

taking any kind of qualifying examination. By 1851, however, the Admiralty required that every man entering the navy had to pass a full medical as well as a written examination. Furthermore, nominations for entering cadets were no longer made predominately by individual captains or Admirals, but rather by the Admiralty itself, with the minimum age requirement set at 12. After the Naval College closed in the 1830s, there was no formal training school for young officers until 1857. Then HMS *Illustrious* in Portsmouth was initially used to train naval cadets for a period of one year before they went to sea, but by 1859 a larger vessel was needed and the school was moved to the *Britannia*.

NUMBER OF SAILORS & OFFICERS IN THE ROYAL NAVY, 1849–52

Rank	Number
Flag Officers	
Admirals	50
Vice-Admirals	63
Rear-Admirals	117
Captains	806
Commanders	1307
Lieutenants	2523
Seamen	150,000
Total	**154,866**

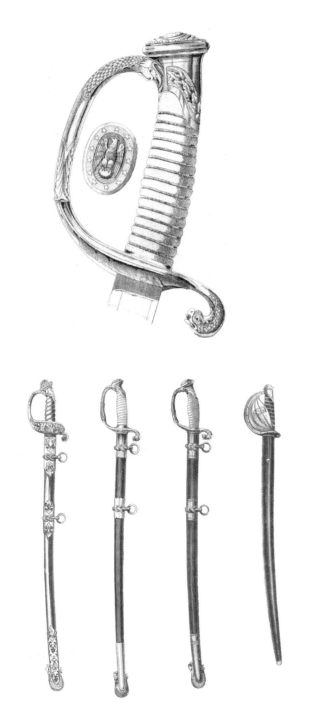

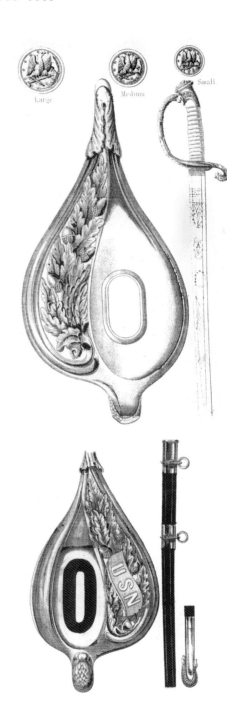

Above left, above right and below: Regulation swords listed in the 1864 illustrated catalogue of Civil War military goods. (Dover Pictorial Archives Series)

Regulation swords listed in the 1864 illustrated catalogue of Civil War military goods. (Dover Pictorial Archives Series)

Above, right and below:
Hilt of the only official
regulation Confederate
naval sword. (Virginia
Historical Center)

Fighting Swords

Throughout the remainder of the nineteenth century commissioned officers of the Royal Navy continued to carry the M1827 as their regulation fighting sword as well as their dress sword. Alterations were made, however, as some officers carried a version with an open half-basket hilt. In 1846 the Royal Navy improved the M1827 by replacing the traditional pipe-back blade with a stronger flat-backed version manufactured by the Wilkinson Sword Company of London and described as:

> *The hilt solid, half-basket guard, with raised bars and crown and anchor badge, lion head back-piece, white fish-skin gripe, bound with three gilt wires; outside length five inches and three quarters; inside length four inches and a half. The blade slightly curved, thirty-one inches and a quarter long, and one inch and three eights wide at the shoulder with a flat back, and the blade ground hollow, to within eleven inches of the end, with a double-edged spear point.*[46]

Officers of the Royal Navy carried this improved sword well into the twentieth century. With such similar swords carried by both commissioned and warrant officers, ornamentation was a visible way to distinguish rank and to express the wealth, prestige and affiliations of the owner. The hilt and blade itself could not be altered, but the scabbard could. Frequently when an officer received a promotion he would have a new more elaborate scabbard produced to accompany the sword he already owned.

Between 1847 and 1856, Flag Officers were allowed to carry a curved sword with Mameluke hilt, similar to those carried by General Officers of the Army and American Marines. The only distinguishable difference was a crown and fouled anchor on the langet. The hilt was made of polished ivory with a hole for the sword knot, and the quillons were shaped as Royal Crowns. The blade was slightly curved, flat-backed, and decorated with oak leaf and acorn decorations. Even after official regulations prohibited the wearing of this sword, some admirals still carried it up to the end of the century.

Southern officers of the US Navy faced a dilemma on the eve of the Civil War, when they had to decide to whom their loyalty belonged, their nation or their home state. Officers stationed or living in the north but with family in the south had the difficult task of deciding whether to take up arms against their own family members. Between 1860 and 1861, many chose their home states and resigned from the Navy. On 29 January 1861 Lieutenant F.B. Renshaw of the US Navy wrote to the Pensacola Naval Yard, discussing the resignation of his commander:

> ... *The veteran commodore declared with deep emotion that although he had served under the flag of the United States in sunshine and in storm for fifty years, loving and cherishing it as he did his heart's blood, he would strike it now, together with the blue pennant, the insignia of his present command, rather than fire a gun or raise his sword against his countrymen, especially in circumstances like the present, when he was without means of defending his position and when an attempt to do so would result in a useless loss of life and destruction of property.*[47]

At first the government did not penalise these men for their decision, but by the outbreak of the war they were seen as deserters and traitors. In the Confederate 'navy', officers who were use to commanding large warships were placed in charge of a makeshift marine of converted merchant ships and other small vessels. Not all men resigned, however; if nothing else, the Union could offer pay and ranks not possible to the Confederacy, which did not even have a navy in 1861. By the end of the war, both the Confederate and Union navies had roughly the same number of officers.

OFFICERS IN THE UNION AND CONFEDERATE NAVIES, 1865[48]

Union	1550
Confederate	1000

NAVAL OFFICERS WHO RESIGNED FROM THE US NAVY, 1860–1

Captains	93
Commanders	127
Lieutenants	351
Surgeons	69
Engineers	247
Gunners	47
Midshipmen	267
Total	**1201**

The background of naval officers in the 1860s was greatly different from those of their predecessors. Officers of the US Navy had learned their craft by going to sea at an early age and working their way up the ranks. By 1845, the Navy Department had established a naval academy in Philadelphia to train officers, later moved to Annapolis, Maryland (during the war, the academy briefly moved to Rhode Island for safety). No longer trained exclusively at sea, students spent four years learning in classrooms, supplemented by summers onboard a vessel. Cadets learned tactics, and gained valuable experience with guns and swords. By 1863, the Confederacy established their own naval academy in Richmond, Virginia, in order to train officers.

If the backgrounds of officers changed during this period, the one factor that remained the same was the symbolism that officers associated with swords. In fact, at no other time does there seem to be as strong an association between sword and honour, as during the American Civil War. On 4 May 1863, in a report to Commodore Barney, Lieutenant Cushing, of the US Navy wrote:

Acting Master's Mate Fader says that when the rebel artillery opened, the officer commanding the howitzer supports ran so fast that he let fall his sword, looking over his shoulder at it, but not daring to stop to pick it up. Mr. Fader, thus deserted, drove the enemy back, picked up the sword, and secured the retreat of his gun. When he reached the fort, the officer asked him for the sword, which was returned with the remark that 'officers should not use their legs at the expense of their honor.'[49]

There are numerous accounts of commanders relinquishing their swords after an enemy captured their ship. On 12 January 1863 the Mississippi Squadron captured the CSS *Pontchartrain* at Arkansas Post. Afterwards First Lieutenant Dunnington sent his sword to its commander, David Porter.[50] The commander of Fort Hindman likewise relinquished his sword to Porter later that month.

In some cases, however, officers refused to relinquish their swords, as with the destruction of the CSS Governor Moore, under the command of Beverly Kennon. In the early hours of 24 April 1862 the *Governor Moore* and other vessels anchored near Fort Jackson when the Union's Mississippi Fleet (consisting of 15 vessels plus a flagship under the command of Flag Officer David G. Farragut) entered the area, initiating a three-hour chase up the river. By six in the morning,

CSS *Alabama*. (Naval Historical Center)

Commander Kennon, realising the hopelessness of his situation, called for the men to set fire to their ship. He and five wounded men boarded the USS *Oneida*, where the captain demanded his sword. Kennon refused stating, 'I would never present the hilt of my sword to any man,' and proceeded to throw it overboard.[51]

Commander Kennon was not the only officer to refuse the demand for his sword. In 1864 General Richard L. Page surrendered Fort Morgan, but when asked for his sword he adamantly argued that he had none to give. Rear-Admiral David G. Farragut knew otherwise and called General Page's comment 'childish'.[52]

In 1852 the Navy Department commissioned a new fighting sword to replace the M1841. A number of officers – including rear-admirals, commanders, flag officers, lieutenants, warrant gunners, warrant boatswains, chief engineers and assistant surgeon – were among those required to wear this sword for both service and full dress. It was modelled directly after the US Army Staff & Field officer's sword, issued in 1850. The pommel was the Phrygian helmet style with an American eagle atop a cable with 13 stars surrounding it. Designers decorated the knuckle bow with a dolphin, scales, and fins, and the counterguard with an open work oak leaf design and inscribed with 'U.S.N.' The quillon terminated in the head of a sea monster. The grip was wood covered sharkskin with 16 twists of copper wire.

Like the M1841, the blade of the M1852 was slightly curved and single-edged, with a false edge. The obverse featured an American shield superimposed on a fouled anchor, an oval of stars, a naval trophy with trident and lances, and a pennant inscribed 'U.S.N.'. The reverse was decorated with an eagle on a naval gun carriage, a fouled anchor and a cable entwined about an oak spray. The scabbard was black leather with three brass mounts two encircled by cable and the third by a dolphin.

After 1862 the so-called 'officer cutlass' appeared. It is the same style and form as the M1861 cutlass for the enlisted men, but decorated with the letters 'USN' cut out of the guard. Other examples had elaborate floral designs above and below the letters. The hilt was gilded rather than brass, and the grip wound with gilt wire. Sometimes the manufacturer embellished the pommel with a floral motif. There is some debate among historians regarding this particular sword type. Some argue that officers adopted the M1861 as a sturdier fighting weapon. While that is possible, it is more than likely that junior officers who could afford a better weapon chose it as a means of distinguishing themselves from the enlisted men.

Even after being supplied with a standardised pattern, however, manufacturers and officers still tried to incorporate their own ideas, particularly in the area of ornamentation. Fighting swords tended to be consistent with the regulations, but most officers would have a second version that was far more ornate for their dress sword. Such officers as Commodore Charles Stewart ordered the M1841 but embellished

it with gold and jewels. The decorations on the scabbard are the same as the regulation model, only in relief not etched. On Admiral Farragut's sword, the obverse side is not engraved with the standard symbols, but rather the goddess of liberty, an American eagle with ribbon in its beak, and bears the words 'Liberty', and 'N.P. Ames, Cutler', and 'Springfield' in three lines. The reverse side features similar designs, except a warrior is substituted for the goddess of liberty, and the legend, flanked by anchors reads 'J. Armstrong/ U.S. Navy'.

Confederate naval officers carried a wide variety of swords to sea. Many wore the M1852 sword they had carried while in the US Navy. Others preferred Confederate army swords such as the staff & field officer's sword. After the outbreak of the war, however, the Confederate Navy Department issued its own regulation sword for officers loosely based on the M1852 officer sword. Instead of a Phrygian helmet, the pommel and backstrap look like a dolphin/sea monster. The guard was of the half-basket style with a hinged counterguard. In place of the acorn motif on the guard, there is the Confederate coat-of-arms (two crossed cannons and a fouled anchor) surrounded by a cotton plant. The grip was wood covered with sharkskin. The blade was slightly curved, single-edged, and had one fuller.

Presentation swords

After the 1840s, the custom of presenting swords to US naval officers who had performed heroic acts increased in popularity. The government, however, no longer gave presentation swords exclusively as in previous times. Other organisations such as states, cities, towns, fraternal organisations and military societies presented them to those that they felt were worthy recipients. Furthermore, between 1860 and 1870, there were no fewer than 25 manufacturers or distributors of presentation swords, the most famous

Raphael Semmes, commander of the CSS *Alabama*. (Naval Historical Center)

being Tiffany & Company out of New York. Some of the other more notable ones were Ames Manufacturing Company; Schuyler, Hartley, and Graham; Horstman Brothers and Company; Bailey and Company; A. W. Spies, Shreve, Stanwood and Company; Staderman and Shapter; William Rose and Sons; and Ball, Black and Company.[53]

In the United States, Union naval officers primarily received presentation swords. Lieutenant Stodder, for example, received two presentation swords for his part in the battle between the *Monitor* and the *Merrimack*, the first battle between two ironclads and a turning point in American naval history. In 1864, Tiffany donated a naval sword valued at $2000 to the United States Sanitary Commission.[54] The public was to decide who received the sword, either Admiral David G. Farragut or Commander Rouan. Admiral Farragut received it. The sword had a silver grip in the form of an eagle with outstretched wings, and the letters 'U.S.N.' engraved into the shell of the guard that curved outwards in the form of a rope with intertwined oak leaves and acorns. The quillon was in the form of Neptune's head. The scabbard was decorated with anchors bound by oak leaves and inscribed with 'Defend thee, Heaven and thy Valor.' Other presentation swords, however, were inspired in style and form by those used as fighting and dress swords. The Naval Academy in Annapolis, Maryland possesses numerous examples of the M1852 manufactured from higher quality materials or encrusted with jewels.

The City of London presented a sword to Raphael Semmes, commander of the CSS *Alabama* in 1864, the only sword given to a Confederate naval officer. The blade was inscribed:

Presented to Captain Raphael Semmes, C.S.N. by officers of the Royal navy and other friends in

England as a testimonial of their admiration of the gallantry with which he maintained the honour of his country's flag and the fame of the Alabama in the engagement off Cherbourg, with a chainplated ship of superior power [USS Kearsage], armament, and crew. June 19th 1864.

Engravers decorated the rest of the blade with floral designs, a crown over an anchor and the Confederate flag. The hilt was made of silver and similarly decorated with nautical and nationalistic symbols. The knuckle bow was in the shape of a winged figure, possibly Nike, the ancient goddess of victory, holding a shield and sword. Floral decorations surrounding an oval medallion cover the grip. In the medallion, the Confederate and British flags were crossed below a star, and above the motto 'Peace and Friendship'. Nautical decorations on the hilt include an anchor and ship's wheel. The scabbard is elaborately decorated with nautical, nationalistic, and classical designs. Both sides were covered with floral motifs (flowers, leaves, corn, palm trees), surrounding cannons, anchors, flags, Alabama's state seal, and a figure of a woman holding a trident and wearing a helmet, perhaps Athena, the ancient goddess of 'civilised' warfare.

* * *

From 1793 to 1865, the Royal and US navies evolved and expanded, and as they did the corps of officers likewise changed. In Britain, the heroism exemplified at the dawn of the nineteenth century by men such as Horatio, Lord Nelson and Lord Cochrane was never fully duplicated. There were two main causes for the generational differences

amongst officer. First, men no longer learned their trade purely by going to sea, but rather attended formal training schools in theory as well as practice. Second, between 1815 and 1865, the Royal Navy remained largely unchallenged at sea. No longer were there large epic battles as seen in Nelson's time. Ships of the navy were primarily used for protecting Britain's commercial interests abroad, and in the suppression of piracy and the slave trade. In the United States, the most significant difference between older and younger officers was their upbringing. Older officers, such as Stephen Decatur Sr. and John Barry, had been British citizens, younger ones such as Stephen Decatur Jr., were strictly Americans. Although both groups were patriotic and courageous, the younger officers stood out because of their fighting prowess, and faith in America as an autonomous and great nation in its own right. The fighting, dress and presentation swords they carried frequently exemplified their beliefs and esteem for their mother country.

The period 1840–65, was also a time of rapid change in naval technology and tactics. As steam engines, explosive shells and iron hulls replaced wooden sailing ships, the need for boarding actions and the use of edged weapons for personal protection declined. It was during this time that the use of a sword as a symbolic object began to surpass its practical value as a weapon. Fighting, dress and presentation swords became more elaborate, reflecting the owner's wealth, rank and affiliations. Furthermore, during no other time can the association between sword and honour be seen so clearly as the emphasis placed upon it by Confederate and Union naval officers of the American Civil War.

CHAPTER 4

Officer Sword Decorations

The Royal Navy of the late nineteenth century was the product of a long and rich heritage dating back to at least the sixteenth century. Immersed in tradition, the officers carried with them the culture, social structure and ideology of British society. Similarly, the development of England's North American and West Indian colonies in the seventeenth century owed a great deal to the Old World, but also much to the innovations and developments produced in the New. When the colonists left England, they did not just take their personal property; they carried English culture, social structure and ideology with them as well. Historians can view these trends in the highly ornate swords used by British and American naval officers from the Revolutionary War through to the American Civil War.

From the eighteenth through the early nineteenth centuries, both the Board of Admiralty and the American government allowed officers to carry any brass mount cut-and-thrust sword as their fighting or dress weapon. This allowed for greater variation and individuality in the decorations used, and consequently the personal tastes and attitude of naval officers affected the rise and fall in the popularity of certain symbols. However, the British Board of Admiralty, introduced the first regulated officer swords in 1805, with revisions in 1825 and 1827. Although regulations were issued in 1797, America did not introduce detailed regulation swords until the 1840s.

In Britain after 1805, even presentation swords

were no longer unique in shape and design. After the introduction of the first regulation sword in 1805, they were commonly more elaborate versions of the regulation sword itself. American designers, however, did not plan for presentation swords to be used as weapons and embellished them to the point of impracticality as weapons, especially in the 1860s and after.

For this book, more than 350 swords from private and museum collections were examined. They were divided into two groups – presentation and officer – with the officer category further divided into fighting and dress swords. Fighting and dress swords fit into one group because it can be hard to distinguish between the two: there are highly ornate fighting swords and very plain dress swords. The total number of symbols examined was 4580, broken down into 90 motifs for officer swords, and 109 for presentation swords. The symbols found on American officer fighting and dress swords fell into six categories: animals, floral/foliage, nationalistic, nautical/maritime, plain and weapons. Symbols on British swords were grouped into twelve categories: animals, figures, floral/foliage, instruments, miscellaneous (beads, orbs, geometric patterns, plain or scrolls), classical mythology, nationalistic, nautical/maritime, religious and weapons. All presentation symbols fell into the same categories as British officer swords, with the addition of heraldic and symbols depicting profession.[1]

Comparison of symbol popularity on American and British naval officer fighting and dress swords, 1775–1865.

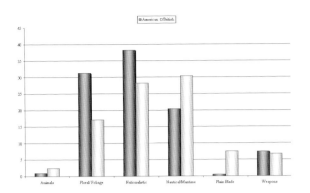

Comparison of symbol popularity on American and British presentation swords, 1775–1865.

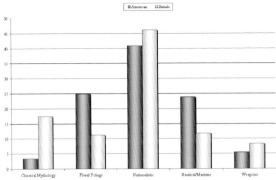

Symbol popularity on American naval officer fighting and dress swords, 1775–1865.

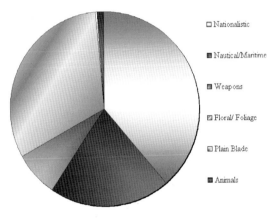

Symbol popularity on American naval officer presentation swords, 1775–1865.

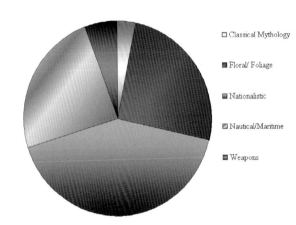

Symbol popularity on British naval officer fighting and dress swords, 1775–1825.

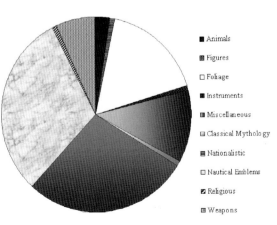

Symbol popularity on British naval officer presentation swords 1775–1825.

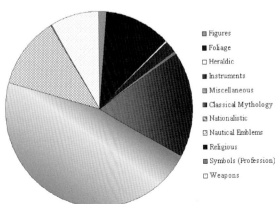

Nationalistic symbols

The majority of symbols found on British officer and presentation swords are related to nationalism. These included crowns, figures, heraldic emblems, lions and royal ciphers. The crown has been the traditional symbol of sovereignty almost since the dawn of civilisation, and the Georgian and the St. Edwards are the two most commonly encountered versions on eighteenth and nineteenth century swords. Similarly, the association between lions and monarchs dates back centuries. Regarded as regal and majestic they are commonly depicted as the rulers of the animal kingdom.

POPULARITY OF NATIONALISTIC SYMBOLS ON BRITISH OFFICER AND PRESENTATION SWORDS, 1775–1865

Symbol	Percentage
Crown	32.13
Lion	31.66
Royal Arms	10.29
Royal Cipher	8.26
Britannia	6.8
Rose	4.67
Motto	3.74
Shamrock	1.5
Sceptre	0.47
Unicorn	0.32
Thistle	0.16

In 1603 King James VI of Scotland succeeded Elizabeth I to the throne of England. Shortly after ascending to the throne, the King commissioned a new coat of arms for the country, which is frequently found on swords manufactured in the nineteenth century. The dominant figures are an English lion and a Scottish unicorn. Up to 1603, the Scottish Royal Arms had been two unicorns supporting a shield, and

Above left: Royal Coat of Arms on regulation naval officer sword. (Annapolis Naval Academy Collection)

Above right: Lion-head pommel. (Author's Collection)

the English Arms used a variety of animals but most frequently the lion. In a symbolic gesture King James combined both into one emblem to indicate the unification of England and Scotland. The unification was poignant as both creatures were considered as king of beasts. The lion was seen as a symbol of majesty, bravery and strength that ruled through might, while the unicorn was seen as a symbol of purity and strength that ruled through harmony.

In the 1603 coat of arms, the lion wears a St. Edwards crown atop its head and the unicorn wears the Crown of Israel around its neck. Both figures stand erect supported by a banner inscribed *Dieu et Mon droit*. French for 'God and my [birth] right', it has been used by the British monarchy since the twelfth century. In 1198 King Richard I used the phrase as a password during the Battle of Gisors, and later to justify his right to rule. In the following centuries, English rulers continued to use the motto as an expression of their belief that they were preordained by God to rule and therefore could be challenged by no man. The unicorn's crown is chained to the words *Mon Droit* and refers to the biblical birthright given to Ephraim, which, like the crown to which it and the Unicorn is chained, can never be removed.

A rose, thistle and shamrock surround the banner as national symbols of England, Scotland and Ireland respectively. The rose was adopted as England's emblem after the War of the Roses (1455–85). The red rose of the House of Lancaster and the white rose of the House of York were combined to make the Tudor Rose when Henry VII of Lancaster married Elizabeth of York, thereby ending 30 years of fighting for control of the English throne. The thistle has been used for centuries as a heraldic emblem of strength and protection. Indigenous to Scotland, it is a large weed-like plant with spiny leaves and a purple head. The first official use of the thistle as a royal badge was in 1474 when James III used it on the back of coinage. The shamrock is a three-leaf plant similar to a clover and is indigenous to Ireland. In ancient times the Druids regarded it as a sacred plant because the leaves formed a triad, a mystical number in the Celtic religion. In the fifth century St. Patrick used the shamrock to illustrate the doctrine of the Holy Trinity when he introduced Christianity to the nation. Together the rose, thistle and shamrock signify the monarchy, military and church.

On the coat of arms, the lion and unicorn hold a heraldic shield. Divided into four quadrants, the first and fourth contain the three leopards of England, which was the coat of arms of Richard I (1189–99). The second quadrant contains the rampant lion of Scotland, which was a Scottish emblem of the monarchy. Legend records that William I was given two lions by a knight returning from the crusades, and liked the creatures so much that he had one depicted rampant on his armour. The third quadrant of the shield contains the harp of Ireland. The oldest official symbol of the nation, the harp first appeared on heraldic arms during the reign of Henry VIII. The four quadrants together depict the unification of the British Isles.

A blue garter inscribed with the Order of the Garter's motto, *Honi soit qui mal y pense* ('Evil [or Shame] to him who thinks it so') encircles the shield. Inspired by the legend of King Arthur and the Knights of the Round Table, Edward III established the order in 1348 as a society, fellowship and college of knights. Membership was very exclusive, consisting of the Sovereign and 25 Knight Companions. The garter was a small strap used to attach pieces of armour together, and might have been used as a symbol of binding the members together in common brotherhood. A royal crown sits atop the garter and indicates the power of the monarchy.

Other emblems found on British swords include Royal ciphers, such as those of King George III (1760–1820), King George IV (1820–30), King William IV (1830–7) and Queen Victoria (1837–1901). Another symbol is the figure of Britannia, which dates back to Roman times and is the female personification of Britain, armed with a shield, trident, and helmet.

POPULARITY OF NATIONALISTIC SYMBOLS ON AMERICAN OFFICER AND PRESENTATION SWORDS, 1775–1865

Symbol	Percentage
Eagle	28.76
E Pluribus Unum	26.16
American Shield	18.64
Star	12.14
Federal Eagle	8.53
Liberty	1.73
Liberty Cap	1.45
Motto	1.16
United States Arms	1.00
Phrygian cap	0.29
Victory	0.14

As on British weapons, the majority of symbols examined on American officer swords were associated with nationalism. This included eagles, shields, figures of victory or liberty and stars. After 1780 eagles became popular decorations in the United States. The rise in popularity of eagle design correlated with the adoption of a coat of arms by the Continental Congress in 1782.[2] Soon after the eagle was established as the national emblem, it was widely adopted as a decorative and patriotic motif on many objects, including furniture, clocks, coins and especially military equipment.[3] In 1782, Charles Thomson, the designer of the Great Seal, described the symbolism of the emblem:

[The shield] is composed of a chief [upper part of the shield] and pale [perpendicular band], the two honorable ordinaries [figures of heraldry]. The Pieces, paly [alternating pales], represent the several states all joined in one solid compact entire, supporting a Chief, which unites the whole and represents Congress…. The colors of the pales are those used in the flag of the United States of America; White signifies purity and innocence; Red, hardiness and valor, Blue, the color of the Chief signifies vigilance, perseverance, and justice.[4]

The dominant figure on the seal's obverse is an American eagle, shown with wings outstretched, a shield with 13 stripes across the breast, and in its beak a ribbon bearing the motto *E Pluribus Unum* ('out of many, one'). The shield is attached to the eagle's breast without any apparent support to denote that the United States of America should rely on its own virtue. The eagle holds an olive branch in its right talon, and a cluster of 13 arrows in its left. The eagle's head faces toward the olive branch to emphasise that the United States would rather live peaceably than be at war.

The olive branch was first associated with the dove that carried an olive branch to Noah's Ark. According to Greek legend, Athena, the goddess of 'civilised' warfare and wisdom, planted the first olive tree on the Acropolis.[5] A wreath of olive leaves upon his head protected Hercules, and for bravery in battle, Roman soldiers were rewarded with crowns of olive branches.[6] Since olives provide oil for lamps, they are associated with light, and the cleansing power of olive oil suggests purification.[7]

Right: 1782 American Great Seal designed by Charles Thomson. (Author)

Far right: American nationalistic symbols on a sword belt, 1860–5. (Virginia Historical Center Collection)

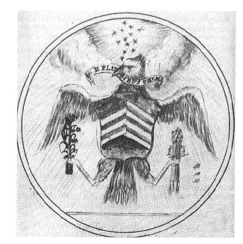

On officer swords the eagle's head commonly faces in the direction of the arrows to symbolise warfare. The arrows are reminiscent of the 'fasces', a bundle of rods with a protruding axe blade borne before Roman magistrates as an emblem of official power.[8] In fact, the bundle of arrows in Charles Thomson's original drawing of the Great Seal depicts them in an alignment very similar to fasces. Infinitely stronger than a single rod, the unbreakable nature of a bundle of arrows is seen as a symbol of the power to wage war.

A cluster of 13 five-pointed stars surrounded by a glory (*ie*, the area where the sun is shown breaking through the clouds) appears above the eagle. The circle of stars was meant to symbolise the first 13 colonies. More were added as new states were created, but this tradition ceased after 16 in 1815.[9] After 1801 the use of a ribbon with the words *E Pluribus Unum* emerged on American swords. Symbols of unity were abundant during the 1770s and 1780s, and this motto was well known to eighteenth-century Americans. It appeared in London's *Gentleman's Magazine*[10] and was used on the title pages printed for annual volumes. There are also examples of eighteenth century swords carried by British naval officers that bear this motto.

Floral decoration

Oak leaves and acorns are also traditional symbols used on both British and American swords dating to the eighteenth and nineteenth centuries. These symbols fall into the floral/foliage category and appeared on 31 per cent of American officer swords and 25 per cent of American presentation swords. On British swords, they appear on 16 per cent of fighting/dress weapons and 9 per cent of presentation swords. Up to the mid-1800s, English warships were built of oak; a hard dense wood that was so strong sailors said England was 'protected by a wall of oak'.[11] Similarly, an officer was said to have a heart of oak, meaning he had strength, integrity and

Federal eagle decoration commonly found on blades of the mid- to late nineteenth century. (Author)

Above: Athena-head pommel from the presentation sword given to Sailing Master John Percival for capturing the *Epervier* on 29 April 1814. (Annapolis Naval Academy Collection)

Above centre: Federal eagle on presentation sword given to Midshipman James Bliss for his participation in the battle on Lake Erie on 10 September 1813. (Annapolis Naval Academy Collection)

Above left: Federal eagle decoration on the guard of John A. Dahlgren's sword. (Annapolis Naval Academy Collection)

Left: Oak leaf motif. (Annapolis Naval Academy Collection)

Left: Stars and oak leaf decoration. (Annapolis Naval Academy Collection)

Above: Mermaid design found on 1812 presentation swords. (Annapolis Naval Academy Collection)

Right: Boat decoration on Stephen Decatur Jr.'s presentation sword. (Annapolis Naval Academy Collection)

Right Nautical motif on Stephen Decatur Jr.'s presentation sword. (Annapolis Naval Academy Collection)

dependability,[12] and in the early nineteenth century, there was an increase in the use of oak leaves on uniform collars.[13]

Nautical and maritime motifs

Almost 26 per cent of all British swords examined and 44 per cent of American had some type of maritime emblem. In the later quarter of the eighteenth century, first hilts, then blades, began to appear with nautical motifs. The first was the fouled anchor, which was an anchor with entangled cable. Other symbols included parts of a vessel, equipment, weapons, aquatic animals and mythological creatures associated with the sea.

PERCENTAGE OF NAUTICAL/MARITIME SYMBOLS ON AMERICAN AND BRITISH OFFICER AND PRESENTATION SWORDS, 1775–1865

| | Percentage | |
Symbol	UK	US
Anchor	14.72	6.01
Anchor – Fouled	35.02	28.42
Boarding Axes	0.65	2.07
Boarding Pikes	5.33	13.27
Buoy	1.3	0
Cannon	4.6	8.29
Cannon-Sword-Pike Motif	0.13	2.48
Cutlass	0.13	0
Dolphin	6.51	0.41
Dolphin Fin and Tail	4.42	2.69
Fish	2.86	0.84
Mast	0.65	1.46
Mermaid	5.33	1.46
Naval Scene	0.52	2.07
Naval Trophies	6.25	5.39
Poseidon/Neptune	0.65	1.46
Quadrant	0.27	0
Rigging	0.13	0
Rope	2.34	9.55
Sailor	0.13	0
Sails	0.13	3.33
Sea Horse	0.13	0
Sea Monster	0.52	0
Shells	2.34	0
Ship	0.52	0.21
Trident	4.42	10.59

Fouled anchors appeared in naval heraldry during the Elizabethan period, but had been associated with maritime tradition since the time of the Ancient Greeks. In England, the fouled anchor as a naval insignia started with Lord Howard of Effingham's seal.[14] He was Lord High Admiral of

England when the Spanish Armada was defeated in 1588. At this time, the personal seal of a great officer of state was often adopted as the seal of his office.[15] When this office became part of the present Board of Admiralty, the seal was retained on buttons, official seals, and cap badges. Even today, the fouled anchor remains the official seal of the Board of Admiralty. In the eighteenth century, the US adopted the symbol from England, but more than likely chose it for artistic purposes, as there was no real positive association for Americans. The lower deck often referred to a fouled anchor as 'the sailor's disgrace', a sentiment which many felt could be extended to its holder. For a sailor there were few things worse than an anchor that could not be retrieved. Today, the fouled anchor has been so integrated into the mind of Americans that when one sees the symbol, one automatically thinks of the navy.

Like the fouled anchor, dolphins have been used as maritime symbols since antiquity because they were thought to be good luck, brought fair weather and good winds, and were repellers of sharks. The Royal Navy began using the dolphin in 1796 with its peak in popularity occurring between 1801 and 1805. The US Navy began using the dolphin in the eighteenth century, but it did not become popular until the M1852 regulation officer sword.[16]

Tridents were used principally on American officer swords and British presentation swords. The trident was the symbol of Neptune/Poseidon, the god of the sea in classical mythology. Before going to sea, a sacrifice was first made to him for a safe voyage.[17] On American swords, the trident conveyed that the United States had become a sea power, able to compete with the European powers. The use of a mast instead of a flagpole meant that the navy could stand up to adversity. A mast was much stronger than a flagpole, and on land, some flagpoles were actually designed like masts because they could resist stronger winds without breaking.[18] Battle-axes appeared only on British swords, and were possibly

Far left: Designs including maritime motifs on the scabbard of Lieutenant John C. Parker's sword. (Annapolis Naval Academy Collection)

Left: Fouled anchor design found on many slotted hilts of the early nineteenth century. (Author)

Right: Fouled anchor etched on the blade of a M1841 regulation sword. (Annapolis Naval Academy Collection)

Far right: Fouled anchor in high relief on the scabbard of Lieutenant John C. Parker's sword. (Annapolis Naval Academy Collection)

used because of their important role in protecting a ship from fire. On swords of the US Navy, American shields would be added, on the British, the Union Jack appears.

Of the total number of swords examined dating between 1775 and 1865, 6.77 per cent of British and 7.46 per cent of American contained some type of naval trophy or scene. Naval trophies were commonly comprised of anchors, flags, foliage, cannons, guns, nautical equipment, pikes and swords. Naval scenes were generally isolated to presentation swords and depicted the battle for which the item was being presented.

Change in use of symbols, 1775–1865

Numerous factors affected the rise and fall in the use of certain symbols. In order to ascertain how symbol popularity changed, swords were analysed in 14 time-spans: 1775–95, 1796–1800, 1801–05, 1806–10, 1811–20, 1821–5, 1826–30, 1831–5, 1836–40, 1841–5, 1846–50, 1851–6, 1857–61 and 1862–5. Some symbols changed in relation to fluctuating sentiments between the United States and Britain between 1775 and 1815. Other symbols fluctuated between peace and wartime, and yet others changed as the views of naval officers evolved between 1775 and 1865.

During the first two periods (1775–95 and 1796–1800), nationalistic symbols such as crowns and royal arms were at the lowest point of their popularity on British naval officer swords. Nautical emblems such as anchors and trophies, on the other hand were the most popular at 27.8 per cent. In the 1770s and 1780s, Britain was locked in a struggle with its American colonies. The long and arduous war, which ended with the colonies winning their independence, certainly affected popular consensus regarding the monarchy and government. The American Revolution was promptly followed by the

war with France in 1793, and Napoleon's initial success in conquering most of Europe affected symbol popularity.

In America between 1775 and 1800, a variety of

Naval scene engraved on the obverse of 1812 presentation swords. (Annapolis Naval Academy Collection)

new symbols appeared on American officer swords as the popularity of decorated blades rose. Despite the hostility between America and Britain during the mid- to late eighteenth century, some symbols were English in origin, such as lion-head pommels, fouled anchors and oak leaves. Many, in fact, continued in use on American swords until the end of the 1800s. Others were not associated with any political or geographical theme, including floral designs, geometric shapes, and nautical motifs such as anchors, masts, sails, tridents and boarding weapons.

By the mid-1790s, symbols and decorations on US naval officer swords changed dramatically as the United States formed its standing navy with its own identity. Before the 1780s, the typical officer sword was either a hunting or small sword, with decorations inspired by the weapons carried by officers of the Royal Navy. As relations deteriorated between the two countries, the United States looked less and less to Britain for inspiration in decorating its swords and supplanted British symbols such as the lion with other more patriotic emblems. During this time, European cutlers in England and Germany began to produce weapons specifically for American tastes and decorated with eagles, American shields and stars.

By the third period (1801–05), there was a marked shift in the type of decorations found on British swords as nationalistic symbols increased dramatically to surpass the use of nautical emblems. This shift followed a period of significant naval victories such as the Battle of Cape St Vincent and the Battle of the Nile. British subjects frequently read of the exploits of officers such as Lord Nelson and St Vincent who achieved spectacular victories over French and Spanish vessels. To the public the superior fighting tactics and naval leadership appeared to be rapidly winning the war for Britain.

As in Britain, nationalistic symbols, such as

eagle-head pommels, stars and American mottoes reached the peak of popularity in America. The use of such nautical emblems as fouled anchors, tridents, and boarding pikes, also remained popular. This correlates with the end of the Quasi-War with France in 1800, and the beginning of the Tripolitan War with the Barbary States.

Although still troubled at times, US and British views towards each other improved after 1800, coinciding with a period when the American Navy recorded few impressments.[19] Furthermore, between January 1802 and August 1803, US officers stationed in the Mediterranean registered no complaints regarding the British in their correspondence, probably because the short-lived Peace of Amiens meant that the Royal Navy was not on a war footing.[20] However, in October 1803 several British citizens on the US Brig *Siren* (16 guns) volunteered for Royal Navy service.[21] Four months later, while chasing an enemy corsair, the USS *Philadelphia* ran aground. To avoid being imprisoned by the enemy, Captain William Bainbridge and 140 crewmembers petitioned Lord Nelson to claim them as British subjects.[22] Lord Nelson refused and the Barbary pirates imprisoned the men until June 1805.

From 1806 to 1810 nationalistic symbols dropped slightly on British swords as maritime, animal and foliage designs supplanted them in popularity. After 1805 there no longer appeared to be an end in sight to the war with France, and Lord Nelson, the nation's hero, had been killed at the Battle of Trafalgar. Furthermore, Anglo-American relations deteriorated dramatically. The nadir of this decline occurred in 1807 with the *Chesapeake–Leopard* incident in which the Royal Navy impressed four sailors off the US frigate. When news spread of how an American warship had been humiliated in an American bay, there arose a great outcry by the public against Britain that spread to

Eagle atop a cannon design engraved on Stephen Decatur's presentation sword. (Annapolis Naval Academy Collection)

Washington and beyond. At this time there was a marked increase in the use of such American nationalistic symbols as federal eagles, American shields and figures of Liberty.

Between 1810 and 1820 the appearance of royal crowns and lions, British symbols of sovereignty, steadily decreased as decorative motifs on blades and hilts. Fighting two wars on multiple fronts proved taxing on the English public and military who became increasingly disillusioned with the government. The use of animal designs such as fish, dolphins and birds continued to increase, reaching the zenith of their popularity. The use of nautical emblems also continued to increase from 22.9 to 26.9 per cent, and foliage designs such as acanthus, oak, and laurel leaves jumped dramatically from 10.49 to 18.1 per cent. After 1815 American nationalistic designs also saw a marked decrease in use as the War of 1812 with Britain ended in a stalemate.

By 1821 the use of animal and foliage designs on British swords dropped as nationalistic and nautical emblems increased. Moreover, nautical emblems reached the pinnacle of their popularity between 1821 and 1825 at 51.5 per cent. In 1827 the government issued a new regulation sword containing these motifs, which is still carried by naval officers in full dress uniform today. The sword itself continued to use the traditional nationalistic symbols found on the M1805 and M1825. The lion-head pommel was maintained but a half-basket hilt decorated with Royal Crown and fouled anchor was added. The blade was ornately decorated with floral and geometric designs, including oak leaves and acorns. Other designs included the Royal Arms, a crown, and nautical symbols such as the fouled anchor. Most officers were generally acquiescing to using a more ornate version of the regulation weapon as their dress sword. Besides the differences in decoration allotted by the Board of Admiralty,

commissioned officers distinguished themselves from warrant officers by the elaborate decorations used to adorn the scabbard of their fighting sword.

After the Board of Ordnance issued a new regulation sword in 1827, British officers generally adhered to the rules for the hilt and overall shape. Some, however, altered the engravings on the blade. Throughout the 1820s up to 1836, nationalistic symbols continued to increase in popularity, while nautical emblems dropped dramatically from 51.5 to 20.6 per cent. Foliage designs continued to increase during this time and the use of weapons (boarding axes, pikes, cannons, guns and swords) increased to 18.9 per cent. In 1839 Britain entered into the first of two Opium Wars with China. Correlating with this is a slight decrease in nationalistic symbols from 39.4 to 34 per cent.

By the 1840s, however, these symbols steadily increased in popularity, perhaps due to Britain's victory over the Chinese in 1842. In 1854 Britain joined other European powers in a conflict with Russia known as the Crimean War, and in 1856 entered into the second Opium War with China. As in the 1830s, the popularity of nationalistic symbols initially decreased in popularity at the onset of these conflicts only to increase dramatically by the end of the decade. By 1865 the popularity of symbols such as the crown, royal arms, lions, roses, thistles, shamrocks and figures of Britannia was at an all-time high of 80 per cent.

In the United States, regulation swords before 1840 were only described in text form. In 1841, the US Navy issued the first regulations that fully illustrated the intended sword, leaving little room for interpretation. While designing it, the navy took into consideration the popularity of certain symbols and incorporated them into the new design. The eagle-head pommel, which had been rising in popularity since the Revolutionary War, was maintained, with plumage extending one third of the way down the backstrap (some officers, however, extended the plumage down the entire length). The government maintained the popular 'reverse-P' knuckle bow and decorated it with oak leaves and acorns. The grip was bone carved into different diamond and geometrical shapes. The quillons contained acorns and oak leaves, and hinged oval guards were on either side of the hilt. The obverse guard was decorated with crossed branches of three oak leaves each and two acorns. The reverse guard was plain. The blade was engraved with three designs: a circle of stars, a fouled anchor, and an oak leaf/acorn spray. These three designs also adorned the scabbard.

In 1852 the navy designed a new sword still carried by officers in full dress uniform today. In designing it, there was a marked increase in the use of nationalistic symbols. The eagle-head pommel was replaced with the Phrygian pommel and decorated with an eagle atop a cable and surrounded by stars. Although acorns and oak leaves were replaced with dolphins on the knucklebow, the guard was still decorated with them and the letters 'U.S.N' were added. Unlike the blade of the M1841, which had three repeated symbols, the M1852 was ornately decorated. Among floral and geometric designs, numerous nautical and nationalistic symbols were added. The obverse side of the blade was decorated with the American shield in front of a fouled anchor, a circle of stars, a naval motif or 'trophy' consisting of a triton, a flag with the letters 'USN', axes, and a mast. The reverse was decorated with an eagle atop a cannon, a fouled anchor, a ribbon with 'USN' on it, and a cable. The scabbard was adorned with cables and a dolphin.

The Confederate Navy designed its own sword not long after 1861. The inspiration for this weapon was clearly a mixture of the M1827 British officer sword and the American M1852, although it contained numerous symbols that can be seen as nationalistic to the Confederate states. The dolphin/sea monster replaced the lion-head pommel, and the solid half-basket guard was decorated in relief with cotton and tobacco plants and the naval coat-of-arms (two crossed cannons behind a fouled anchor). The blade was decorated with cotton plants on one side and tobacco on the other as well as the Confederate flag and the naval coat of arms. The scabbard was plain, with the exception of two twisted snakes wrapped around the drag in place of the dolphin found on the M1852.

Traditions of the sword

Over the centuries, many ceremonies and traditions have arisen around the sword. As discussed earlier, when a ship was captured or a battle lost, the sword of the commander was relinquished to the victor. In the Royal Navy, when an officer was court-martialled, his sword was placed on the table with the point of the blade facing him if found guilty, and away if innocent (if guilty, his sword was later ceremonially broken). This practice may date to the Middle Ages, when an executioner preceded a prisoner from the court to the prison. Depending on the direction of the axehead, the public was informed if the person was guilty or innocent.[23]

In a sword salute, a solider brings the sword's hilt to the chin and then extends it to arm's length. The movement of the hilt to the mouth originated with the Crusades, when a solider kissed the crucifix-shaped hilt of his sword before going into battle. The sword held at arm's length originally acknowledged a superior, and to let the tip touch the ground was a sign of submission.[24]

There is also the tradition of preserving swords of famous people. There are numerous museums in England that preserve any sword presented to or carried by Lord Nelson as collection centrepieces. In February 1855, the US Congress convened to discuss the matter of establishing a memorial for General Andrew Jackson's sword as a 'national treasure of patriotism'.[25] Mr Lewis Cass, Senator from Michigan, argued that Andrew Jackson's sword should be preserved as a memorial alongside George Washington's sword because he had:

> ... never been brought into contact with a man who possessed more native sagacity, more profundity of intellect, higher powers of observation or greater probity of purpose, more ardor of patriotism, nor more firmness of resolution ....[26]

He argued that by exhibiting this sword, the American public would see:

> ... another legacy of departed greatness, another weapon from the armory of patriotism ... be carried back by association to those heroes of early story, and will find their love of country strengthened, and their pride in her institutions and their confidence in her fate and fortunes increased, by this powerful faculty of the mind – a faculty which enables us to triumph over the distant and the future, as well as over the stern realities of the present, gathering around us the mighty dead and the mighty deeds that excite the admiration of mankind, and will ever command their respect and gratitude.[27]

* * *

In the last century, there has been little work done to analyse the material culture of naval weapons. Historians argued that nothing could be learned from artefacts that could not be learned from the documentary record alone. Other scholars, including Thomas J. Schlereth and Ivor Noël Hume, argued that artefacts could be extremely beneficial in revealing information about past cultures.[28] Naval officer swords used from 1775–1865 provide such an example. The designs chosen to adorn hilts and blades reflected the political and international conditions at the time as well as the desire to emphasise each country's superiority at sea. As the United States' relationship with Britain rose and declined, so too did the popularity of British and American symbols.

Up to 1865, the popularity of symbols in the Royal and American navies rose and fell in connection with times of war and peace and in connection with the fashions of the day. After the introduction of regulation swords, the level of individuality found in weapons decreased steadily as officers commonly carried the regulation pattern as their fighting and dress sword. Furthermore, after the 1820s British presentation swords were commonly modelled on the regulation sword of the time. In America, however, cutlers continued to produce presentation swords that were unique in design and lavishly decorated.

CHAPTER

Manufacturers of Naval Edged Weapons, 1775–1865

Edged weapons of the eighteenth and nineteenth centuries were the creation of talented cutlers, most of who were born into families with a long history of sword manufacturing. Whether running individual smith shops, operating as part of a cottage industry, or working as an employee at a large manufacturing centre, these men drew on a rich heritage dating back centuries to when the first lavishly-decorated swords were produced by highly skilled smiths in ancient times. By 1800 England had successfully employed the expertise of individual smiths to establish blade centres at Birmingham, Sheffield and Enfield. Rather quickly these centres were able to produce blades and hilts of a high quality, although they did not hold the prestige associated with the better-known centres of Solingen or Klingenthal. Similarly, American cutlers achieved a level of efficiency and quality in edged weapon production that rivalled Europe. No less than 75 American contractors produced edged weapons for the US Navy from 1797 to 1815, and 53 between 1840 and 1865.[21] Most, however, were engaged in fulfilling government contracts, requiring officers to obtained personal weapons from abroad. Three main areas in Europe supplied not only the blades themselves, but also the hilts. These centres were Solingen in Germany, Klingenthal in France, and the English centres of Birmingham, Sheffield and Enfield.

Solingen

Located on the Austrian border at the convergence of the Inn, Isar and Danube rivers, Passau was Germany's most significant blade centre throughout the Middle Ages. By the fourteenth century, however, almost all the natural resources of the area had been depleted. Furthermore, Germany was under constant threat of attack from its neighboring countries, and Passau's close proximity to France concerned the local ruling princes. During this period France suffered from political instability and pressures generated by the Hundred Years War. In order to protect German interests, should France invade, it was decided to build a new blade centre further from the border. The city of Solingen located in Westphalia, near the River Rhine, was chosen as the new location. It was ideal in many ways: set on a hill bordering the Wupper River, the city's surrounding terrain provided an abundance of natural resources (iron ore, timber for charcoal, and water to power the grindstones) and protection from foreign invasion. Furthermore, it was only 20 miles north-east of Cologne, Germany's richest trading centre of the time.

The blade centre in Solingen consisted of two sectors controlled by powerful guilds. The first were the numerous iron and steel forges that were responsible for blade and scabbard manufacture. Once the blade was completed, the second sector, a cottage industry, was responsible for the manufacture of hilts. The grinders' and temperers' guilds were formed in 1401 and the sword smiths' guild in 1472.

By the beginning of the seventeenth century, the city of Solingen consisted of 188 houses with about

Map of American manu-
facturing centres.
(Author's Collection)

MN

WI

MI

IA

ME

VT

NH

NY

Chelmsford
Chicopee
MA   Springfield   Hingham
Canton   Hartford
Berlin   Middletown
Fishkill
CT
New York
RI
Boston

IL

IN

OH   Zanesville

PA

Pittsburgh   Nicholson Township
York   Philadelphia
NJ

MO

WV

MD   Baltimore
Washington D.C.
Georgetown

DE

KY

VA   Richmond

Norfolk

TN   Nashville

NC

AR   Memphis

Kenansville

SC   Columbia

Atlanta

Charleston

MS   AL   GA   Macon

Columbus

Natchez

LA

Mobile

New
Orleans

FL

● Location of Sword, Axe, and/or Pike Manufacture

▲ Location of Sword Manufacture

■ Location of Boarding Pike Manufacture

1200 inhabitants, most of whom were engaged in sword production. The quality and artistry of Solingen swords were renowned all over Europe, and the city enjoyed a period of wealth and prosperity. Solingen blades were in such high demand that unscrupulous manufacturers would put Solingen markings on their own blades in order to sell them.[2]

This peaceful era was not to last. For the next 300 years, Germany was in a constant state of turmoil as wars broke out and the country suffered from social unrest. In 1618 the Thirty Years War broke out, resulting in a civil war between the German principalities as they took up arms for or against the Hapsburg rulers. Most of the country was devastated by the conflict, and Solingen suffered a recession that took more than 100 years to recover from.

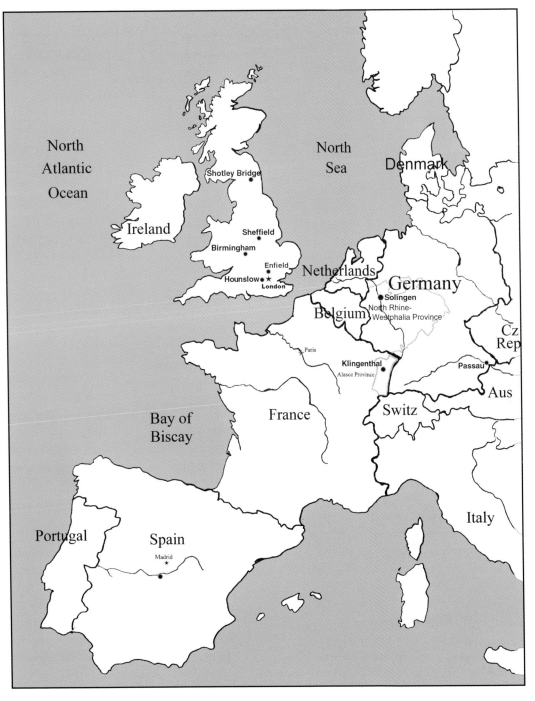

Map of European manufacturing centres. (Author's Collection)

For centuries, England, France, and other countries attempted to entice Solingen blade-makers to emigrate in order to build their own cutlery industries, but the German guilds held such power that only the most inept manufacturers emigrated to England. Anyone wanting to leave the guild had to first work at another trade for five years in another city before they could leave. Throughout the seventeenth century, however, religious conflicts between Catholics and Protestants made life in Germany very difficult for anyone desiring religious freedom. It was during this time that France and England were able to acquire blade-makers with the necessary skills to create successful weapons industries.

By the beginning of the eighteenth century, Solingen was again one of the prominent leaders among European sword producers. For the next 200 years, such families as Braf, Eickhorn, Clauberg, Kirschbaum, Knecht, Peres and Wayersberg controlled blade manufacturing during the late eighteenth and early nineteenth centuries.[3] By 1800 Germany was suffering from effects of the French Revolutionary and Napoleonic Wars, Bonaparte's strategic and commercial policies severely restricting Solingen's exports. In their absence, the blade-making centres in Sheffield and Birmingham, England, were quick to occupy this gap in the world market. After the war, Solingen's industry grew rapidly but never really reached its pre-war levels, having lost a large number of its export markets in England and America. By the 1860s Solingen was in the process of mechanising most of its production as industrialisation spread throughout Europe. By the end of the century it had shifted its focus away from regulation swords towards dress and presentation pieces, surgical instruments, scissors and knives.

Klingenthal

In France, King Louis XV established a blade centre that he hoped would rival Solingen in 1729, and tasked M. d'Angervillers, a former Intendant of Alsace, to find the perfect location. He finally decided on Klingenthal ('valley of the blades'), located in the eastern province of Alsace, near the German border. The city was chosen because of its natural resources: iron ore and timber for charcoal, close proximity to the Ehn River, which would provide the necessary water supply for powering the forges and foundries, and the natural barrier formed by the mountains.

A year later, the King granted Henri Anthès a 30-year commission to establish the necessary facilities and act as Director. Anthès already had a forge in Rothau ('Red Meadow') and was ideally suited for this task. In 1731 the Manufacture d'Armes Blanches d'Alsace commenced operation with ten skilled workers from Solingen, Germany.[4] Unlike Solingen though, which relied on a dispersed cottage industry for much of the work, the manufacturing plant in Klingenthal consisted of a central location housing a mill, workshops and lodgings for the men.

The early years of the factory were marked by unrest and disorganisation. Anthès died in 1733, followed by a rapid succession of directors ending when the factory closed around 1751. Reopening in 1755, accommodations for the director and his staff were constructed. The factory was also renamed Manufacture de Klingenthal, a name which can be found on thousands of blades produced throughout the nineteenth century.

In the beginning, Klingenthal was managed through a franchise or royally granted monopoly, but managed by an entrepreneur (a civilian businessman) who was responsible for the financial operations of the factory. His main responsibilities included making sure the factory had the necessary supplies of iron, charcoal and manpower to fill any government contract. He also paid the workers' salaries and ensured that all government contracts were followed properly. For every order, he received 20 per cent of the profits.

After the Revolution in France, the title of entrepreneur was changed to director. The director was still responsible for weapon production, but he was no longer a civilian, rather a senior artillery officer was appointed for two to four years and assisted by a staff of four officers.[5] It was his responsibility to maintain quality control and monitor the speed of production so that orders would be filled promptly. He reported to the army and earned no more than an officer's salary.

From 1797 to 1815, Napoleon's armies occupied Germany, and Solingen fell under French control. He quickly abolished the trade guilds' monopolies in Solingen and combined the efforts of Klingenthal and Solingen so that French workers for the first time had full access to the secrets of Solingen manufacture. This had a tremendous effect on blade manufacturing – the most impressive blades made during the eighteenth and nineteenth centuries came from this union.

After all the troubles of the eighteenth century, Klingenthal prospered in the nineteenth. This was due, in part, to the direction and management of the Coulaux family. The Coulaux brothers successfully applied for the job of director in February 1801 and, for the next 35 years, they ran the factory as a government facility. In 1836, however, the French government – fearing instability in Europe and not wanting to depend on acquiring their weapons from a factory so close to the borders of Germany – relinquished Klingenthal as a government facility and moved the manufacture of French regulations swords to a new centre established in 1818 at Châtellerault near Poitiers.[6] The Coulaux family was allowed to purchase the factory as a civilian business, which they managed until the Manufacture de Klingenthal closed in 1962. No longer under the constraints of the government, they produced agricultural equipment such as scythes and sickles as well as dress and presentation swords for individuals and local and international retailers.

British manufacturers

Despite continual importation of blades from Germany, Britain established its own cutlery industry during the late eighteenth century. Historically, the dependence on foreign blades was viewed as an embarrassment and a threat to national security by a succession of British monarchs who worked to keep sword prices down in order to preserve the home market against foreign competitors. Between 1722 and 1865, 457 cutlers manufactured or assembled edged weapons in England, Scotland and Ireland, with forty years as the average span of a particular business.

AVERAGE LIFESPAN OF ENGLISH CUTLER BUSINESSES, 1722–1865

Location	Years
London	45.25
Plymouth	35
Portsmouth	34.56
Provincial	25.41
Ireland	15.05

By the nineteenth century, British attempts to create a domestic industry had borne fruit. To accomplish this, it had at first relied on families from Solingen. In the 1620s a sword factory was established in Hounslow utilising the knowledge and skills of these Solingen craftsmen. Before this effort, weapons were bought in parts from large manufacturing centres and assembled by local smiths, predominantly in London. In 1687 a factory was established in Shotley Bridge in Northumberland, which survived until 1832, but England did not achieve any true success until the factories at Sheffield and especially Birmingham were established in the eighteenth century.

Based in the western midlands of England, Birmingham was well situated in terms of natural resources and a high-quality labour base to develop into one of the most important blade factories in England. Established in the beginning of the eighteenth century, it would be another 50 years, however, before blades of exceptional quality would be produced at Birmingham. By the end of the century the factory entered a period of unprecedented growth caused by the French Revolution and later the Napoleonic Wars. Urgently, Birmingham worked to meet the needs of the government, especially after 1806 when their access to Solingen blades was cut off by Napoleon's invasion of Germany. Within five years, Birmingham had the capabilities to produce, hilt and finish officer swords that were equal in quality and craftsmanship to those imported and mounted by London smiths. This zenith of British blade manufacturing was short-lived, however. The War of 1812 cut off the American market, and after 1815 and the end of the Napoleonic Wars the demand for large quantities of edged weapons came to an abrupt end. It would be almost 20 years before government contracts for edged weapons would resume. Furthermore, Solingen re-entered the market, regaining most of its previous influence. Birmingham fell into a depression that it never really recovered from.

In 1804 the government established the Royal Small Arms Factory at Enfield Lock to provide weapons for the British army, and a swordsmith in 1823. However, whenever needed – such as during the build-up of arms in the 1840s – the factory at Enfield would manufacture naval cutlasses, so long as it did not interfere with other orders.

Most officers carried weapons manufactured in France or Germany. To acquire them they went to local dealers who imported the complete swords and blades or imported only the blades and hilts and manufactured the scabbards domestically. During the eighteenth century, an English swordmaker's shop doubled as a factory and showroom.[7] Owners assembled, but rarely made, swords in these shops.

NOTABLE ENGLISH SWORDSMITHS OF THE EIGHTEENTH AND NINETEENTH CENTURIES

Name	Years of Operation	Location
John Harvey	1748–1800	Birmingham
Thomas Gill & Company	1774–1826	London
Thomas Hadley & Company	1781–1808	Birmingham
James Woolley & Company	1785–1825	Birmingham
J.J. Runkel	1795–1808	London
George Reddell	1802–21	Birmingham
Henry Osborn	1803–19	Bordesley
Thomas Craven & Company	1803–20	Birmingham
Tatham & Egg	1803–60	London
Thomas Bates	1814–20	Birmingham
John Cooper	1815–20	Birmingham
John Heighington	1847–79	Liverpool

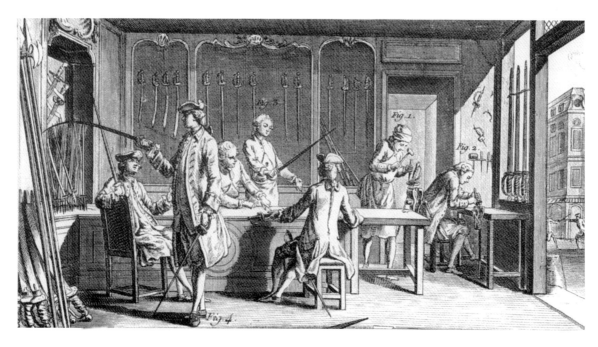

Eighteenth-century view of a sword shop. (Dover Pictorial Archives Series)

Decorations and wire wrappings were the only things added to small sword hilts.

Officers of the Royal Navy depended on London sword-cutlers who imported blades from the Continent and hilted them locally. Of these cutlers, J.J. Runkel was one of the more prominent dealers in London during the late eighteenth/early nineteenth centuries. German by birth, Runkel emigrated to England in the 1790s, where he imported German blades to sell to the British navy and army. In 1772 Henry Nock, a noted sword cutler and gunsmith set up his shop in London. Amongst his apprentices was his son-in-law James Wilkinson, who was later to become his partner. In 1805, Wilkinson inherited the shop upon Nock's death. From the beginning, the Wilkinson Company had a reputation for producing high-quality weapons, and manufactured blades for the government and ceremonial and presentation swords for officers.

In 1824 James' son Henry took over, moving the business next door to the Board of Ordnance offices in Pall Mall. In order to address customer concerns regarding the brittleness of British blades, Henry developed a testing machine called the Eprouvette in 1844 to test stress levels in his blades. After rigorous testing, each blade that passed was marked and certified, guaranteeing that either Henry or his manager John Latham had personally tested the weapon. In 1846 all naval officer swords were refurbished with Wilkinson blades. By 1858 Henry's health had deteriorated and John Latham assumed control of the business. Of the two-dozen sword cutlers active in England during the eighteenth and nineteenth centuries, only the Wilkinson Sword Company exists today.[8]

American manufacturers

In America, officers also purchased their swords from dealers. One of the first dealers was Edward Pole of Philadelphia, who imported boarding pikes and

DEALERS PROVIDING THE NAVAL REGULATION SWORDS

Dealer	Location	Years
Hilborn & Hamberger	New York, NY	1861–5
William H. Horstmann & sons	Philadelphia, PA	1852–93
N. S. Meyer Inc.	New York, NY	1875–1992
John Miller & Co.	New York, NY	1863–8
Abner W. Pollard & Co.	Boston, MA	1863–6
Jacob Schuyler, Marcellus Hartley, & Malcom Graham	New York, NY	1854–65
Seebass Brothers	New York, NY	1863–5
Benjamin Shreve, Henry B. Stanwood & Co.	Boston, MA	1861–9
James S. Smith & Co.	New York, NY	1864–91
Adam W. Spies & Co.	New York, NY	1839–65
Francis Tomes Jr., Benjamin Son & Robert C. Melvain	New York, NY	1859–65
William Wall, Thomas K. Stephens & Co	Washington, D.C.	1863–75

cutlasses from 1760 to 1800. Between the 1840s and 1860s, most dealers were located in New York, with around 13 providing regulation naval swords. One of the more famous was William H. Horstmann & Sons of Philadelphia, who between 1843 and 1893 provided a complete line of United States regulation swords and presentation pieces. They also offered silver-hilted swords manufactured by Tiffany & Company.

From 1798 to 1837 Nathan S. Starr was the main provider of cutlasses and sabres for the United States government. He was born in April 1755 to Joseph and Pricilla Starr in Middletown, Connecticut. Starr began blacksmithing at the age of 14 when he was apprenticed to a European-trained smith. His master was also an expert swordsmith and taught Nathan his craft. By the age of 22, Starr was manufacturing edged weapons for the Connecticut Militia. The earliest record of this appears in the accounts of state expenses held by Commissioner Elijah Hubbard, which reads: '1777, Decr., 9th , To cash paid Nathan Starr's bill for smith work – £4/14/0.'[9]

Starr produced various items, including cart tyres, sleighs, nails, 'common bars' and other hardware from 1777 to 1798.[10] In 1798 he received his first contract to produce 2000 cavalry sabres for the US government at a cost of $5.00 each.[11] This established the N. Starr & Company that would make different types of swords for the military.[12] Historical references to Starr & Sage or Nathan Starr & Co. refer to a brief partnership between Nathan Starr and Francis Sage and his son Wilbert Sage in 1798.[13] The partnership was made to aid Starr's production of the 2000 cavalry sabres ordered by the government, and ended with delivery of the order.

In 1799, Starr made 50 M1797 cutlasses for the 24-gun ship *Connecticut* being built in Middletown, Connecticut. It was, however, not until 18 May 1808

NAVAL EDGED WEAPON CONTRACTS TO NATHAN S. STARR

Date	Weapon Type	Quantity Manufactured
1799	Cutlass	50
1808	Boarding pike	2000
1808	Naval cutlass	2000
1816	Naval cutlass	1000
1816	Boarding pike	1000
1818	Non-commissioned sword	4000
1826	Naval cutlass	2000

that he received his first contract from the US Navy: to manufacture 2000 cutlasses at $2.50 each, and 2000 boarding pikes at $0.75 each.[14] In 1813 Starr relocated his factory to a larger facility on the West River after he received a substantial contract from the War Department.[15] He was then able to produce better-quality weapons because of the additional room, men and equipment.

In 1812 Starr entered into another partnership when his son Nathan Jr. joined the business. He remained in the business after Nathan Sr. died in 1821 and continued operations until the government

discontinued the contract system in 1845.[16] Nathan Starr and his son were among the more prolific manufacturers of naval weapons, but they were by no means the only ones, since there were at least 45 active weapons manufacturers from 1795 to 1815.

The majority of contractors worked out of shops in Pennsylvania. Three of Starr's contemporaries were Lewis Prahl, William Rose, and the company of Mayweg and Nippes. Prahl worked in Northern Liberties, Philadelphia, providing swords for the government before 1782. Although no specimens of Prahl's swords are known to survive, he is listed as a navy contractor for cutlasses until 1800.[17]

William Rose, along with his son Joseph, produced bayonets, cavalrymen's sabres, sergeants' swords and presentation swords. Rose established his factory in Blockley Township, Philadelphia, in 1800.[18] The Roses held several contracts for naval cutlasses and produced 72 presentation swords ordered by Congress for War of 1812 naval heroes. The documents suggest that Rose had been an apprentice of Lewis Prahl. This conclusion is based on 1798 tax records, showing Rose's property as containing a dwelling house, a smith shop, a stone blade mill and a large foot-stone tilt mill along with other structures.[19] The size and nature of Rose's holdings suggest it had been there for some time prior to the census, and may have been purchased

Nathan Starr's Factory, West River, Middletown, Connecticut, *circa* 1813. (Courtesy of the *Gun Report*, 'America's First Swordmaker', by James D. Spina)

from Prahl.[20] Another producer of naval weapons was the Philadelphia company of Mayweg and Nippes, which received a government contract in 1814 for 2000 cutlasses at a cost of $3.00 each.[21]

By the 1840s Nathan Starr was replaced by the Ames Manufacturing Company as the most prolific provider of edged weapons to the United States Navy. When Nathan P. Ames finished his apprenticeship as a blade smith in 1791 he set up a shop in Chelmsford, Massachusetts. His sons, Nathan P. Jr. and James T. Ames learned the craft from him, and in 1829 the shop was moved to Chicope Falls, Massachusetts. In 1831 they received their first government contract, and in 1832, two years before the death of Nathan P. Ames, Sr., the Ames Manufacturing Company, originally called the Chicopee Manufacturing Company) was formed with a capital of $34,000.[22]

Sword manufacturing took place in Cabotsville, Springfield and Chicopee plants. Each location was chosen because of the close proximity to water supplies needed to power the machinery. Springfield, for instance, was located at the intersection of major highways and the Connecticut River as well as nearby supplies for weapon manufacturing. In the 1830s Ames revolutionised how edged weapons were produced when he introduced the process of electro-plating and gilding as a means to compete with the cheap labour of Europe.[23] Electroplating allowed Ames to mass-produce weapons in a shorter period then ever before.

Out of the 13 Confederate States, 53 per cent had edged-weapon centres. Most were located in Virginia and Georgia until 1864, when Atlanta fell to Union troops under General Sherman. For the most part, sword makers concentrated on producing weapons for the enlisted men using either the M1840 or M1860 cutlass model. These makers included the Confederate States Armory in Kenansville, NC; Edmund J. Johnson & Co., and William J. McElroy both out of Macon, GA. Officers obtained their weapons from a few local manufacturers such as Louis Bissonnet of Mobile, AL or Louis Huiman & Brother of Columbus, GA, but more commonly they turned to sword dealers that imported weapons from England. C. Hall of Norfolk, VA, sold M1841 officer swords produced by Joseph Rogers & Son in Sheffield, England. William C. Courtney & Gilbert B. Tennent & Co., imported cutlasses and the Confederate naval regulation sword from the firm Robert Mole & Son in Birmingham, England.

Besides sword manufacturers, there were 15 producers of boarding pikes and axes during the Federal Period. Twelve contractors were located in Pennsylvania or Maryland; the other three were at

NAVAL EDGED WEAPON CONTRACTS TO THE AMES MANUFACTURING CO.

Date	Weapon Type	Amount Manufactured
1841–1846	M1841 Naval Cutlass	6,600
—	M1840 Naval Officer Sword*	0
1852–1853	M1852 Naval Officer Sword	500
1861–1864	M1860 Naval Cutlass	22,000
—	M1862 Naval 'Officer' Cutlass*	0

Although none of these varieties were produced for the government, Ames made them available for individual purchase by officers.

NUMBER OF EDGED WEAPON CENTRES BY TOWN

Atlanta, GA	23
Mobile, AL	10
Charleston, SC	6
Nashville, TN	5
Columbia, SC	22
Natchez, MS	3
Columbus, GA	23
New Orleans, LA	17
Macon, GA	17
Richmond, VA	26
Memphis, TN	8
Kenansville, NC	1

the New York Naval Yard, Boston Naval Yard, and Washington Naval Yard.[24] Daniel Pettibone also produced boarding pikes for the Committee of Defense during the War of 1812.[25] In 1816, he bid on a naval contract for swords and boarding pikes at $3.00 each.[26]

Other manufacturers worked out of or near Philadelphia. Cromel Barney produced pikes for the American Navy in 1797, as did John Coler who received a government contract for 164 naval pikes later that year. Cladius M. Cox worked for Daniel Pettibone making pikes between 1814 and 1815. He also produced 200 boarding pikes for the State of Pennsylvania in 1814. John Harris worked at York, Pennsylvania, and in 1797 obtained a government contract for 300 boarding pikes for the frigates *Constitution*, *Constellation* and *United States*. He also produced boarding pikes for the frigate *Ganges* in 1798.[27]

Not all pike makers were located in Pennsylvania. Some were situated in Baltimore, Maryland, in the period 1797–9. One was Henry Foxall, who made 100 boarding pikes for the ship *Adams* in 1799. John Martin, also in Baltimore, obtained a government contract for M1797 boarding pikes.[28] In 1799, Robert Gill made 100 boarding pikes each for the *Maryland* and the *Chesapeake*.[29] Another contractor was William Smeeton who, like Martin, produced M1797 boarding pikes.

Axe manufacturers are not as well documented as swordmakers or pike makers. Frederick Hoffman, a Philadelphia blade maker from the 1770s onward, received a contract in 1797 to produce boarding axes for the government. He identified his work by 'US Hoffman' on the blade. In 1806 he placed a bid with the US Navy for boarding axes at a cost of $1.00 each; in 1816, he placed another bid, at a cost of $2.00 each.[30]

Other axe makers included Isaac Hoglan from Georgetown, Washington D.C., who placed a bid with the government in 1816 to produce 'battle axes' at $0.95 and boarding axes at $0.75 each. Elijah Brown of Richmond, Virginia, also placed a bid with the government in 1816 to produce axes for the navy at $2.50 each. Private contractors were not the only source for navy weapons. During the War of 1812, the Boston Navy Yard produced 90 boarding axes and pikes for the frigate *Constitution*. The New York and Washington Navy Yards also produced boarding axes and pikes.[31]

United States government inspectors were required to test the shipments of domestic and international blades. The lengthy process was recorded in a letter from Commander John Rodgers to arms inspector Robert Dingie. Dimensions were first compared to the type specimen. Then each blade was struck twice on each of the flat sides and once on the edge with a round, white oak block 1 foot in diameter.[32] The point would then be tested by bending it on the floor in each direction to ensure that it did not break. The inspector carefully examined each blade to ensure that it did not have any flaws, cracks or other imperfections by applying oil to the surface, wiping off the excess, and seeing if the oil revealed any cracks invisible to the naked eye. This was the process used throughout the nineteenth century.[33]

In 1801–02 John McLean inspected military equipment for the New York Commissary of Military Stores. After inspecting them, he stamped each with the letters 'V.IM'. Numerous axes from this period contain his mark. During the War of 1812 Joseph Tarbell inspected naval weapons for the Washington Naval Yard and numerous axes contain the mark 'J.T.' on the blade.[34]

During the period 1798 to 1801 the United States developed a strong small-arms industry due largely to the support of Benjamin Stoddert, who purchased large quantities of naval edged weapons from local smiths. By the end of 1815, there were at least 75 weaponsmiths supplying the US government. These men were skilled at their craft and produced everything from the most rudimentary axes to the most spectacular presentation swords. Many, however, were overwhelmed with government contracts, leaving naval officers to acquire their weapons from abroad. At first swordsmiths produced exact copies of European weapons, but as the industry grew, they developed weapons that were distinctive to the United States including the single-disk cutlass, eagle-head pommel sword and naval boarding axe.

* * *

By the 1840s the number of manufacturers began to dwindle for several reasons. First, the period 1775 through 1815 was marked by almost continual warfare that spurred the need for and development of weapons. During this time, individuals such as Nathan Starr, William Rose and Lewis Prahl and industrial centres in England, Germany and France made weapons to meet the demand. Between 1815 and the 1840s, there was a period of relative peace in which no outside force threatened national security, thus eliminating a need to stockpile weapons. After the 1850s and the Industrial Revolution, large factories capable of mass-producing standardised weapons in shorter periods emerged.

Symbol Categories and Characteristics

Officer Fighting and Dress Swords, 1775-1865	*Officer Presentation Swords, 1775-1865*
ANIMALS	**ANIMALS**
Aigrette	Aigrette
Birds	Birds
Dog-head Pommel	Crocodiles
Dogs	Dog-head Pommel
Dolphin	Dogs
Fish	Dolphin
Goat, Charging	Dolphin fin and tail
Snake	Dove
	Dragon
	Fish
	Goat, Charging
	Horse
	Ram
	Sea Horse
	Snake
FIGURES	**FIGURES**
Figure	Figure
Human Face	Human Face
Human Head Pommel	Human Head pommel
	Warrior with Helmet
FOLIAGE DESIGNS	**FOLIAGE DESIGNS**
Acanthus	Acanthus
Acorn Motif	Acorn Motif
Foliage Design	Bay Leaves
Honeysuckle	Foliage Design
Laureate	Honeysuckle
Laurel Spray	Laureate
Oak Leaf Spray	Laurel Leaf Spray
Olive Pommel	Oak Leaf Spray
Wreath	Olive Branch
	Olive Pommel
	Palm Branch
	Wreath
	HERALDIC
	Coat of arms
INSTRUMENTS	**INSTRUMENTS**
Drums	Drums
Trumpet	Trumpet
Globe	Globe

Officer Fighting and Dress Swords, 1775-1865	*Officer Presentation Swords,1775-1865*
MISCELLANEOUS	**MISCELLANEOUS**
Arc with Rays	Arc with Rays
Beads	Barrel
Geometric Patterns	Beads
Initials	Coronet
Orb	Decorated Scabbard
Ovide	Geometric Patterns
Plain Blade	Initials
Scroll	Orb
	Ovide
	Plain Blade – decorations on hilt
	Scroll
CLASSICAL MYTHOLOGY	**CLASSICAL MYTHOLOGY**
Hercules	Club of Hercules
Hope	Hercules
Poseidon/Neptune	Hercules and the Hydra
Roman Fasces	Hercules and the Nemean Lion
Trident	Hope
Vase – Classical	Mars
	Medusa
	Minerva
	Perseus
	Phoenix arising from ashes
	Poseidon/Neptune
	Roman Fasces
	Thunderbolts
	Trident
	Vase – Classical
	Victory
NATIONALISTIC	**NATIONALISTIC**
American Shield	American Shield
Britannia	Britannia
Circle of Stars	Circle of Stars
Crown	Crown
E Pluribus Unum	*E Pluribus Unum*
Eagle	Eagle
Eagle-head Pommel	Eagle Gripping Arrow and Olive Branch
Eagle Plumage	Eagle Plumage
Federal Eagle	Eagle-head Pommel
Flag	Federal Eagle
Liberty	Flag

Continued on next page

Officer Fighting and Dress Swords, 1775-1865	*Officer Presentation Swords, 1775-1865*	*Officer Fighting and Dress Swords, 1775-1865*	*Officer Presentation Swords, 1775-1865*
Liberty Cap	Liberty	**WEAPONS**	**WEAPONS**
Lion	Liberty Cap	Arms & Armour	Arms & Armour
Lion-head Pommel	Lion	Boarding Axes	Arms & Crest
Motto	Lion Headed Sea monster	Boarding Pikes	Axe
Phrygian cap	Lion-head Pommel	Cannon	Boarding Axes
Royal Arms	Mottos	Grenade	Boarding Pikes
Royal Cypher	Phrygian cap	Gun	Cannon
Sceptre	Rose	Grapnel	Cannon-Sword-Pike Motif
Star	Royal Arms	Helmet	Cutlass
Unicorn	Royal Cypher	Shield	Grapnel
United States Arms	Scepter	Spears	Grenade
	Shamrock	Swords	Guns
	Stars		Helmet
	Thistle		Shield
	Unicorn		Spears
	United States Arms		Sword
	Union Jack		
	United States Coat of Arms		

NAUTICAL/MARITIME	**NAUTICAL/MARITIME**
Anchor	Anchor
Anchor - Fouled	Anchor – Fouled
Buoy	Buoy
Mast	Mast
Naval Coat of Arms	Mermaid
Naval Emblems	Naval Coat of Arms
Naval Scene	Naval Emblems
Naval Trophy	Naval Scene
Octant	Naval Trophies
Quadrant	Octant
Rope	Quadrant
Rudder	Rigging
Sails	Rope
Shell	Rudder
	Sailor
	Sails
	Sea Monster
	Shells
	Ship

RELIGIOUS	**RELIGIOUS**
Angel	Angel
Cherub	Cherub
Cross	Cross
Garter	Garter
Shield of David	Shield of David
Star of David	Star of David

	SYMBOLS
	Caduceus (medical)
	Maltese Cross

Notes to Chapters

Introduction

1 William A. Albaugh III, *Confederate Edged Weapons* (New York: Harper & Brothers, 1960); William A. Albaugh III, *A Photographic Supplement of Confederate Swords* (Orange, Virginia: Moss Publications of Orange, 1979); Giles Cromwell, *The Virginia Manufactory of Arms* (Charlottesville, Virginia: The University Press of Virginia, 1975); Ron G. Hickox, *Collector's Guide to Ames U.S. Contract Military Edged Weapons: 1832–1906* (Brandon, Florida: Miracle Printing & Copy Center, 1984); Warren Moore, *Weapons of the American Revolution … and Accoutrements* (New York: Funk & Wagnalls, 1967); George C. Neumann, *Swords & Blades of the American Revolution* (Harrisburg, Pennsylvania: The Stackpole Company, 1973).

2 Claude Blair, *European & American Arms c. 1100–1850* (New York: Crown Publishers, Inc., 1962); H.R. Ellis Davidson, *The Sword In Anglo Saxon England* (Oxford: Oxford University Press, 1962); A.V.B, Norman and Don Pottinger, *English Weapons & Warfare: 449-1660* (New York: Barnes and Noble, 1966); Ewart Oakshott, *The Archaeology of Weapons: Arms & Armor from Prehistory to the Age of Chivalry* (New York: Barnes & Noble, 1960); Ewart Oakshott, *A Knight and his Weapons* (Chester Spring, Pennsylvania: Dufour Editions, Inc., 1964).

3 William Gilkerson, *Boarders Away with Steel: The Edged Weapons and Polearms of the Classical Age of Fighting Sails, 1626–1826 – Tracing their Development in the Navies of England and Northern Europe Through that of the United States* (Lincoln, Rhode Island: Andrew Mowbray, Inc., 1991), pix.

4 P.G.W. Annis, *Naval Swords: British and American Naval Edged Weapons 1660–1815* (Harrisburg, Pennsylvania: Stackpole Books, 1970); Gilkerson, *Boarders Away with Steel*; Harold L. Peterson, *The American Sword: A Survey of the Swords Worn by the Uniformed Forces of the United States from the Revolution to the Close of World War II* (Philadelphia, Pennsylvania: Ray Riling Arms Books Company, 1954).

5 William B. Hesseltine, 'The Challenge of the Artifact', in Thomas J. Schlereth (ed), *Material Culture Studies in America* (Walnut Creek, California: Altamira Press, 1999), pp93-4.

6 Lewis R. Binford, *An Archaeological Perspective* (New York: Seminar Press, 1972), pp23-5.

7 Ernle Bradford, *The Story of the Mary Rose* (New York: W.W. Norton and Company, 1982), pp188-9; A.G. Credland, 'Some Swords of the English Civil War with notes on the Origins of the Basket-Hilt', *The International Journal of the Arms and Armour Society*, vol. 10, no. 6 (December 1982), pp196-205; Colin J.M. Martin, 'The Cromwellian Shipwreck off Duart Point, Mull', in Mark Redknap (ed.), *Artefacts from Wrecks: Dated Assemblages from the Late Middle Ages to the Industrial Revolution* (Oxford: Oxbow Monograph no. 84, 1997), pp167-180.

8 James Ringer, 'Phip's Fleet', *National Geographic*, vol. 198, no. 2 (August 2000), pp73-81.

9 Emily Cain, *Ghost Ships: Hamilton and Scourge: Historical Treasures from the War of 1812* (New York: MUSSON/Toronto, 1983), p3.

Chapter 1

1 Department of the Navy, *Rules for the Regulations of the Navy of the United Colonies of North America*, Naval Historical Center, Washington, D.C., 1775.

2 Gilkerson, *Boarders Away with Steel*, p25.

3 Gunner Stores of the Sloop-of-War *Boston*. September 17, 1832; Military Store Inventory of the Brig *Franklin*. 9 August 1807, National Archives, Washington, D.C.; Outfitting list for the Frigate *United States*, August 28, 1830, National Archives, Washington, D.C.; Armory Receipt for the Sloop of War *Falmouth*, 27 August 1830; Gunners Stores for the *John Adams*, National Archives, Washington, D.C.

4 John L. Cotter and J. Paul Hudson, *New Discoveries at Jamestown: Site of the First Successful English Settlement in America* (Washington, D.C.: National Park Service, 1957), p71.

5 George C. Neumann, *Swords & Blades of the American Revolution*, (Harrisburg, PA: The Stackpole Company, 1973), p257.

6 Gilkerson, *Boarders Away with Steel*, pp25-8.

7 Neumann, *Swords & Blades of the American Revolution*, p257.

8 Daniel R. Headrick, *The Tools of Empire: Technology and Europe and Imperialism in the Nineteenth Century* (Oxford: Oxford University Press, 1981), p87.

9 Neumann, *Swords & Blades of the American Revolution*, p191.

10 Harold L. Peterson, *Arms and Armour in Colonial America, 1526–1783* (New York: Bramhall House, 1956), p92; Jamestown Rediscovery Project, *Halberd*. [Jamestown, Virginia: The Association for the Preservation of Virginia Antiquities, 1997, accessed 3 October 2002]; available from http://www.apva.org/ngex/c9halb.html; Internet.

11 Gilkerson, *Boarders Away with Steel*, p36.

12 Nick Evangelista, *The Encyclopedia of the Sword* (London: Greenwood Press, 1995), pp561-2; Richard F. Burton, *The Book of the Sword* (New York: Dover Publications, Inc., 1884), pp222, 236, 270, 274.

13 Anthony North, 'Eighteenth and Nineteenth Century Europe', *Swords and Hilt Weapons* (New York: Barnes and Noble Books, 1989), pp86- 7.

14 James Gilch Bentonrist, *The Fabrication of Small Arms for the United States Service*, Prepared under the direction of Stephen V. Benét assisted by J.E. Greer, D.A. Lyle and E.S. Allin (New York: Benchmark Publishing Company Inc., 1970), p218.

15 Carlo Panseri, 'Damascus Steel in Legend and in Reality', *Gladius*, vol. IV (1965), p12; Bentonrist, *The Fabrication of Small Arms*, p219.

16 Anthony North, 'Seventeenth Century Europe', *Swords and Hilt Weapons* (New York: Barnes and Noble Books, 1989), p83; J.D. Alyward, *The Small-Sword in England: its History, its Forms, its Makers, and its Masters* (New York: Hutchinson's Scientific & Technical Publications, 1945), p103; Bentonrist, *The Fabrication of Small Arms*, p221.

17 Alyward, *The Small-Sword*, p114.

18 Bentonrist, *The Fabrication of Small Arms*, pp220-1.

19 Wayne Lusardi, 'Shipwrecked Swords: An Examination of Edged Weaponry Recovered from Spanish Colonial Vessels and Archaeological Sites, 1492 – 1733' (M.A. diss., East Carolina University, 1998), p9.

20 Geoffrey Parker, *The Military Revolution: Military Innovations and the Rise of the West, 1500-1800* (Cambridge: Cambridge University Press, 1996), p1.

21 Oakeshott, *A Knight and His Weapons*, p90.

22 Peterson, *Arms and Armour in Colonial America*, p114.

23 Evangelista, *Encyclopedia of the Sword*, p491.

24 *Ibid*.

25 Lusardi, 'Shipwrecked Swords', p17.

26 Bradford, *The Story of the Mary Rose*, pp188-9; Alexandra Hildred, 'The Material Culture of the *Mary Rose* (1545) as a Fighting Vessel: The Uses of Wood', *Artefacts from Wrecks: Dated Assemblages from the Late Middle Ages to the Industrial Revolution* (Oxford: Oxbow Monograph no. 84, 1997), pp59, 69-70.

27 Cotter and Hudson, *New Discoveries at Jamestown*, p70; Allan J. Wingwood, '*Sea Venture* Second interim report – part 2: the artifacts', *International Journal of Nautical Archaeology and Underwater Exploration*, vol. 15, no. 2 (May 1986), pp149–51.

28 Alyward, *The Small-Sword*, p12.

29 *Ibid*.

30 Moore, *Weapons of the American Revolution and Accoutrements*, p125.

31 Peterson, *Arms and Armour in Colonial America*, p75.

32 W.E. May and P.G.W. Annis, *Swords for Sea Service* (London: Her Majesty's Stationery Office, 1970), p9.

33 Peterson, *Arms and Armour in Colonial America*, p271.

34 Evangelista, *The Encyclopedia of the Sword*, p145.

35 *Ibid*.

36 Colonel Robert H. Rankin, *Small Arms of the Sea Services* (New Milford, Connecticut: N. Flayderman and Co., Inc., 1972), p11; Evangelista, *The Encyclopedia of the Sword*, pp286-7; May and Annis, *Swords for Sea Service*, p9.

37 May and Annis, *Swords for Sea Service*, p3.

38 Peterson, *Arms and Armour in Colonial America*, p82; Anthony North, 'From Rapier to Smallsword', *Swords and Hilt Weapons* (New York: Barnes & Noble Books, 1989), p78.

39 James C. Tily, *The Uniforms of the United States Navy* (New York: Thomas Yoseloff, 1964), p18.

40 E. Andrew Mowbray, *The American Eagle Pommel Sword* (Lincoln, Rhode Island: Andrew Mowbray, Inc., 1988), p39; May and Annis. *Swords for Sea Service*, p24.

Chapter 2

1 Brian Lavery, *Nelson's Navy: The Ships, Men and Organisation 1793–1815* (London: Conway Maritime Press, 1989), p317.

2 Donald L. Canney, *Sailing Warships of the US Navy* (Annapolis, Maryland: Naval Institute Press, 2001); Paul H. Silverstone, *The Sailing Navy 1775 –1854* (Annapolis, Maryland: Naval Institute Press, 2001).

3 Samuel Leech, *Thirty Years from Home or A Voice from the Main Deck* (London: H. G. Collins, 1851), pp23–4.

4 Rankin, *Small Arms of the Sea Services*, p7.

5 Leech, *Thirty Years from Home*, p.

6 James P. Delgado, *Encyclopedia of Underwater and Maritime Archaeology* (New Haven, Connecticut: Yale University Press, 1997), p187; Daniel A. Nelson, '*Hamilton & Scourge*: Ghost Ships of the War of 1812' *National Geographic*, vol. 163, no. 3 (March 1983), pp289–300; Gilkerson, *Boarders Away with Steel*, p44.

7 Leech, *Thirty Years from Home*, p72.

8 Rankin, *Small Arms of the Sea Services*, p4.

9 Michael Calvert, A *Dictionary of Battles, 1715–1815* (London: New England Library, 1978), p124.

10 Ernle Bradford, *Nelson: The Essential Hero* (London: Wordsworth Military Library, 1999), pp139–40.

11 Rankin, *Small Arms of the Sea Services*, p4.

12 Daniel D. Hartzler, *Arms Makers of Maryland* (Philadelphia, Pennsylvania: George Shumway Publisher, 1977), p17.

13 James McHenry to Wm John Harris, 10 August 1797, transcript in the hand of James McHenry, National Archives, Washington, D.C.

14 James McHenry to Wm John Harris, 4 May 1797, transcript in the hand of James McHenry, National Archives, Washington, D.C.

15 Armory Receipt for the Sloop of War *Falmouth*, 27 August 1830. National Archives. Washington, D.C.; Gunner Stores of the Sloop-of-War *Boston*. 17 September 1832. National Archives, Washington, D.C.; Gunners Stores for the *John Adams*. National Archives, Washington, D.C.; Military Store Inventory of the Brig *Franklin*, 9 August 1807.

National Archives, Washington, D.C.; Outfitting list for the Frigate *United States*, 28 August 1830. National Archives, Washington, D.C.

16 Rankin, *Small Arms of the Sea Services*, p3.

17 Contract proposal between Frederick Hoffman and United States Navy, 1806, National Archives, Washington, D.C.

18 Francis Bannerman, *Bannerman Catalog of Military Goods 1927* (original manuscript reproduced by DBI Books, Northfield, Illinois: 1930), p209.

19 Rankin, *Small Arms of the Sea Services*, p6.

20 Gilkerson, *Boarders Away with Steel*, p62.

21 Wm John Harris to Samuel Hodgdon, 10 August 1797, transcript in the hand of John Harris, National Archives, Washington D.C.; James McHenry to Wm John Harris 4 May 1797. Transcript in the hand of James McHenry, National Archives, Washington, D.C.

22 Contract Proposals 1816, National Archives, Washington D.C.; James E. Hicks, *Nathan Starr, U.S. Sword and Arms Maker* (Mt. Vernon, New York: James E. Hicks Publishing, 1940), p91.

23 Armory Receipt for the Sloop of War *Falmouth*, 27 August 1830, National Archives, Washington, D.C.; Gunner Stores of the Sloop-of-War *Boston*, 17 September 1832, National Archives, Washington, D.C.; Gunners Stores for the *John Adams*, National Archives, Washington, D.C.; Military Store Inventory of the Brig *Franklin*, 9 August 1807, National Archives, Washington, D.C.; Outfitting list for the Frigate *United States*, 28 August 1830, National Archives, Washington, D.C.

24 Lavery, *Nelson's Navy*, p103.

25 Stephen H.P. Pell, 'American Pole Arms or Shafted Weapons', *Bulletin of the Fort Ticonderoga Museum*, vol. 5 no. 3 (July 1939), p68.

26 Rankin, *Small Arms of the Sea Services*, p15.

27 Gilkerson, *Boarders Away with Steel*, p.

28 Quoted in Leland P. Lovette, *Naval Customs, Traditions and Usage* (Menasha, Wisconsin: George Banta Publishing Company, 1934), p197.

29 *Ibid.*, p79.

30 *Ibid.*; P.R.O. W.O. 47/2579, 30 May 1804.

31 Annis, *Naval Swords*, pp40–1.

32 May and Annis, *Swords for Sea Service*, p79.

33 Robert W. Bingham, 'The Evolution of the American Naval Cutlass', *Museum Notes of the Buffalo Historical Society*, vol. 2, no. 1 (January–March 1953), pp6–7.

34 *Ibid.*

35 Richard H. Bezdek, *American Swords and Sword Makers* (Boulder, Colorado: Paladin Press, 1994), p181.

36 Quoted in Tily, *Uniforms of the United States Navy*, p23.

37 Peterson, *The American Sword 1775 – 1945*, p49.

38 Alfred F. Hopkins, 'Nathan Starr Cutlass of 1808', *Bulletin of the Society of American Sword Collectors*, vol. 3, no. 5 (October 1948), p4;

Harold Peterson. 'The American Cutlass', *Bulletin of the Society of American Sword Collectors*, vol. 3, no. 2 (October 1949), p13.

39 James D. Spina, 'America's First Swordmaker', *The Gun Report* (March 1975), p5; Hicks, *Nathan Starr*, p11; Gilkerson, *Boarders Away with Steel*, pp96–7.

40 Contract Proposals 1814, National Archives, Washington, D.C.

41 Lavery, *Nelson's Navy*, p130.

42 *Ibid.*, p81.

43 Peterson, 'The American Cutlass', p3.

44 Gilkerson, *Boarders Away with Steel*, p101.

45 Robert Edward Gardner, *Five Centuries of Gunsmiths, Swordsmiths, and Armourers, 1400 –1900* (Columbus, Ohio: Long's College Book Company, 1950), pp198, 201, 203.

46 Mowbray, *The American Eagle Pommel Sword*, pp16–18.

47 E.H.H. Archibald, *The Wooden Fighting Ship In the Royal Navy, AD897-1860* (New York: Arco Publishing Company, Incorporated, 1971), pp155–7.

48 Lords of the Admiralty, *The Seaman's Catechism And Instructor in Gunnery, Rifle, Cutlass, and The Armstrong Gun Drill; The mariners Compass; Storm Signals; Hand, Deep Sea, Lead and Log Lines; Stowage of Holds and Stores, &c., &c.,* (London: Simpkin, Marshall & Co., 1850s).

49 Alfred Hutton, *The Sword and the Centuries* (London: Grant Richards, 1901), p348.

50 Donald L. Canney, *Lincoln's Navy: The Ships, Men and Organization, 1861-65* (London: Conway Maritime Press, 1998), pp8–9.

51 Dr. Robert M. Browning Jr., 'The Confederate States Navy Department,' in Dr William N. Still, Jr *The Confederate Navy, The Ships, Men and Organization, 1861-1865* (London: Conway Maritime Press, 1997), p39.

52 Donald L. Canney, 'The Enlisted Sailor,' in *Lincoln's Navy*, p117; Dr. Robert M. Browning Jr. 'The Confederate States Navy Department', p133.

53 United States, Navy Department, *Official Records of the Union and Confederate Navies in the War of Rebellion, Series II, Volume 2, Navy Department Correspondence, 1861-1865* (Washington, D.C.: Government Printing Office, 1894–1922), pp602–56.

54 United States, Navy Department, *Official Records of the Union and Confederate Navies in the War of Rebellion, Series I, Volume 13, South Atlantic Blockading Squadron. From May 14, 1862, To April 7, 1863* (Washington, D.C.: Government Printing Office, 1894 – 1922), pp750.

55 United States, Navy Department, *Official Records of the Union and Confederate Navies in the War of Rebellion, Series I, Volume 5, Operations On The Potomac And Rappahannock Rivers. From December 7, 1861, To July 31, 1865* (Washington, D.C.: Government Printing Office, 1894–1922), pp302–57.

56 United States, Navy Department, *Official Records of the Union and Confederate Navies in the War of Rebellion, Series I, Volume I, Operations Of The Cruisers—Union. From January 19, 1861, To January 31, 1863*

(Washington, D.C.: Government Printing Office, 1894–1922), pp501–51.

57 United States, Navy Department, *Official Records of the Union and Confederate Navies in the War of Rebellion, Series I, Volume 15 South Atlantic Blockading Squadron, From October 1, 1863, To September 30, 1864* (Washington, D.C.: Government Printing Office, 1894–1922), pp505–49.

58 United States, Navy Department, *Official Records of the Union and Confederate Navies in the War of Rebellion, Series I, Volume 15, South Atlantic Blockading Squadron, From October 1, 1863, To September 30, 1864* (Washington, D.C.: Government Printing Office, 1894 – 1922), pp505–49.

59 United States, Navy Department, *Official Records of the Union and Confederate Navies in the War of Rebellion, Series I, Volume 23, Naval Forces On Western Waters, From April 12 To December 31, 1862* (Washington, D.C.: Government Printing Office, 1894–1922), pp417–50.

60 United States, Navy Department, *Official Records of the Union and Confederate Navies in the War of Rebellion, Series I, Volume 23, Naval Forces On Western Waters, From April 12 To December 31, 1862* (Washington, D.C.: Government Printing Office, 1894–1922), pp604–55.

61 United States, Navy Department, *Official Records of the Union and Confederate Navies in the War of Rebellion, Series I, Volume 24, Naval Forces On Western Waters, From January 1 To May 17, 1863* (Washington, D.C.: Government Printing Office, 1894–1922), pp458–99.

62 United States, Navy Department, *Official Records of the Union and Confederate Navies in the War of Rebellion, Series I, Volume 4, Operations On The Potomac And Rappahannock Rivers, January 5 To December 7, 1861* (Washington, D.C.: Government Printing Office, 1894–1922), pp601–54.

63 United States, Navy Department, *Official Records of the Union and Confederate Navies in the War of Rebellion, Series I, Volume 19, West Gulf Blockading Squadron, From July 15, 1862, To March 14, 1863* (Washington, D.C.: Government Printing Office, 1894–1922), pp701–79.

64 United States, Navy Department, *Official Records of the Union and Confederate Navies in the War of Rebellion, Series I, Volume 7, North Atlantic Blockading Squadron, From March 8 To September 4, 1862,* (Washington, D.C.: Government Printing Office, 1894–1922), pp250–307.

65 United States, Navy Department, *Official Records of the Union and Confederate Navies in the War of Rebellion, Series I, Volume 1, Operations Of The Cruisers—Confederate, From April 18, 1861, To December 31, 1862* (Washington, D.C.: Government Printing Office, 1894–1922), pp610–75.

66 May and Annis, *Swords for Sea Service*, p80.

67 *Ibid.*, pp80–6.

68 Hickox, *Collector's Guide to Ames U.S. Contract Military Edged Weapons, 1832 – 1906*, p41.

69 Letter from the Navy Department to James T. Ames, May 18, 1861. In Hickox, *Collector's Guide to Ames U.S. Contract Military Edged Weapons, 1832 – 1906*, p43.

70 *Ibid*, p44.

71 *Ibid*, p45.

Chapter 3

1 Lavery, *Nelson's Navy*, p94.

2 *Ibid.*, p100.

3 *Ibid.*, p88.

4 M.A. Lewis, *A Social History of the Royal Navy, 1793 – 1815* (London, 1960), pp31, 36.

5 Tom Wareham, *The Star Captains: Frigate Command in the Napoleonic Wars* (Annapolis, Maryland: Naval Institute Press, 2001), p94.

6 Quoted in Joseph F. Callo, *Nelson Speaks: Admiral Lord Nelson in his Own Words* (Annapolis, Maryland: Naval Institute Press, 2001), pxvii.

7 Tily, *Uniforms of the United States Navy*, p18.

8 Lovette, *Naval Customs, Traditions and Usage*, p21.

9 *Ibid.*, p19.

10 Tily, *Uniforms of the United States Navy*, p19.

11 Christopher McKee, *A Gentlemanly and Honorable Profession: The Creation of the U.S. Naval Officer Corps, 1794-1815* (Annapolis, Maryland: Naval Institute Press, 1991), p33.

12 Michael A. Palmer, *Stoddert's War: Naval Operations During the Quasi-War with France, 1798-1801* (Annapolis, Maryland: Naval Institute Press, 2000), p14.

13 McKee, *A Gentlemanly and Honorable Profession*, p210.

14 Cyrus Talbot to Silas Talbot, 12 January 1800, transcript in the hand of Cyrus Talbot, National Archives, Washington, D.C.

15 *Ibid.*, p212.

16 McKee, *A Gentlemanly and Honorable Profession*, p403.

17 Charles Lee Lewis, *The Romantic Decatur* (Oxford: Oxford University Press, 1937), p190.

18 William L. Rodgers note, April 1813, quoted in McKee, *A Gentlemanly and Honorable Profession*, p189.

19 McKee, *A Gentlemanly and Honorable Profession*, p403.

20 Quoted in Bradford, *Nelson: The Essential Hero*, p140.

21 First Lieutenant Bartholomew Clinch, to Major Commandant William W. Burrow, 8 June 1799, quoted in Claude A. Swanson (editor), *Naval Documents Related to the Quasi-War between the United States and France: Naval Operations from April 1799 to July 1799* (Washington, D.C.: Government Printing Office, 1936), p318.

22 Captain John Rodgers, U.S. Navy, to Secretary of the Navy, 23 May 1806, quoted in Frank Knox (ed.), *Naval Documents related to the United States Wars with the Barbary Powers: Volume VI, Naval Operations Including Diplomatic Background from May 1805 through 1807* (Washington, D.C.: Government Printing Office, 1941), p432.

23 Tily, *Uniforms of the United States Navy*, p56.

24 Peterson, *The American Sword 1775–1945*, p47.

25 Hickox, *Collector's Guide of Ames U.S. Contract Military Edged Weapons: 1832–1906*, p41.

26 Captain Henry T.A. Bosanquet, *The Naval Officer's Sword* (London: Her Majesty's Stationery Office, 1955), p10.

27 Rankin, *Small Arms of the Sea Services*, p11.

28 Annis, *Naval Swords*, p11.

29 Rankin, *Small Arms of the Sea Services*, p19; Gilkerson, *Boarders Away with Steel*, p117; May and Annis, *Swords for Sea Service*, pp20–1.

30 Gilkerson, *Boarders Away with Steel*, p117; Rankin, *Small Arms of the Sea Services*, p19; Peterson, *The American Sword*, p104–05.

31 Annis, *Naval Swords*, p38.

32 *Ibid.*

33 Bannerman, *Bannerman Catalog of Military Goods, 1927*, p185; Gilkerson, *Boarders Away with Steel*, p119.

34 May and Annis, *Swords for Sea Service*, p29.

35 Annis, *Naval Swords*, p14–15.

36 May and Annis, *Swords for Sea Service*, pp30–5.

37 George Cameron Stone, *A Glossary of the Construction, Decoration and Use of Arms and Armor in all Countries and in All Times* (New York: Jack Brussel Publisher, 1961), p596.

38 Annis, *Naval Swords*, p17.

39 Tily, *Uniforms of the United States Navy*, p50.

40 *Ibid.*, pp273-7.

41 Mowbray, *The American Eagle Pommel Sword*, p51.

42 *Ibid.*, pv.

42 Peterson, *The American Sword*, p189.

44 Annis, *Naval Swords*, p16.

45 Lavery, *Nelson's Navy*, p108.

46 Quoted in May and Annis, *Swords for Sea Service*, p45.

47 Philip Oliver, *Official Records of the Union and Confederate Navies In the War of the Rebellion, Series I—Volume 4, Operations In The Gulf Of Mexico. November 15, 1860, To June 7, 1861* (Washington D.C.: Government Printing Office, 1894–1922), pp58–99.

48 *Ibid.*

49 Philip Oliver, *Official Records of the Union and Confederate Navies In the War of the Rebellion, Series I—Volume 8 North Atlantic Blockading Squadron, From September 5, 1862, To May 4, 1863* (Washington D.C.: Government Printing Office, 1894–1922), pp750–803.

50 Philip Oliver, *Official Records of the Union and Confederate Navies In the War of the Rebellion, Series I—Volume 24 Naval Forces On Western Waters, From January 1 To May 17, 1863* (Washington D.C.: Government Printing Office, 1894–1922), pp100–53.

51 Philip Oliver, *Official Records of the Union and Confederate Navies In the War of the Rebellion, Series I— Volume 18 West Gulf Blockading Squadron. From February 21, 1861 – July 14, 1862*, (Washington D.C.: Government Printing Office, 1894–1922), pp278–335.

52 Philip Oliver, *Official Records of the Union and Confederate Navies In the War of the Rebellion, Series I— Volume 21 West Gulf Blockading Squadron. From January 1 To December 31, 1864*, (Washington D.C.: Government Printing Office, 1894–1922), pp504–59.

53 Jay P. Altmayer, *American Presentation Swords* (Mobile, Alabama: The Rankin Press, 1958), p29.

54 *Ibid.*

Chapter 4

1 Once the groups and characters were chosen, the program Microsoft Excel was used to evaluate connections between British and American naval swords. The experimental and control groups were matched based on hilt and blade styles. No significant differences were found between the two groups on these matching variables. Of the original sample of 90 characters, six had to be removed from the American group and 17 from the British group because there were no examples that fell within the dated categories. All symbols were counted once for each time they appeared, on either the blade or hilt, with the exception of floral and oak leaf spray designs, which were counted once for every motif that appeared rather than individual flower or leaf.

2 Ralph E. Arnold, 'Early American Eagle Head Swords, Part I', *Arms Gazette* (October 1975), p11.

3 J. Franklin Jameson, *Dictionary of United States History 1492 – 1899* (Boston, Massachusetts: History Publishing Company, 1899), p237.

4 Charles Thomson, 'Remarks and Explanations, of the Great Seal of the United States,' reproduced in Paul Foster Case, *Great Seal of the United States* (Washington, D.C.: Government Printing Office, 1976), p6.

5 Philip Mayerson, *Classical Mythology in Literature, Art, and Music* (New York: Scott, Foresman and Company, 1971), pp169–70.

6 Timothy R. Roberts, *Ancient Civilizations: Great Empires at Their Height* (New York: Smithmark Publishers, 1997), pp132–5.

7 Mayerson, *Classical Mythology*, p32.

8 Stone, *A Glossary of the Construction, Decoration and Use of Arms and Armor in all Countries and in All Times*, pp71–2.

9 Jameson, *Dictionary of United States History*, p237.

10 *Ibid.*, p210.

11 David Wilson, interview by author, phone conversation, Annapolis, Maryland, 10 September 1999.

12 *Ibid.*

13 Tily, *Uniforms of the United States Navy*, pp57–64.

14 US Navy, *Navy Uniform History* (Washington, D.C.: Naval Media Center, 1995), p1.

15 *Ibid.*

16 Peterson, *The American Sword 1775–1945*, pp161–2.

17 Mayerson, *Classical Mythology*, pp98–101.

18 David Wilson, interview by author, phone conversation, Annapolis, MD, 10 September 1999.

19 Dudley W. Knox (ed.), *Naval Documents related to the United States Wars with the Barbary Powers: Volume IV, Naval Operations Including Diplomatic Background from April to September 6, 1804.* (Washington, D.C.: Government Printing Office, 1941).

20 Dudley W. Knox (ed.), *Naval Documents related to the United States Wars with the Barbary Powers: Volume II, Naval Operations Including Diplomatic Background from January 1802 through August 1803* (Washington, D.C.: Government Printing Office, 1941).

21 Dudley W. Knox (ed.), *Naval Documents related to the United States Wars with the Barbary Powers: Volume III, Naval Operations Including Diplomatic Background from September 1803 through March 1804* (Washington, D. C.: Government Printing Office, 1941), p120.

22 First Lieutenant John Johnson to Lieutenant Colonel Commandant William W. Burrows, 24 January, 1804 in Dudley W. Knox (ed.), *Naval Documents related to the United States Wars with the Barbary Powers: Volume III, Naval Operations Including Diplomatic Background from September 1803 through March 1804* (Washington, D.C.: Government Printing Office, 1941), p357.

23 Lovette, *Naval Customs, Traditions and Usage*, p26.

24 *Ibid.*, p27.

25 United States Congress, *Addresses on the presentation of the sword of General Andrew Jackson to the Congress of the United States, delivered in the Senate and House of representatives, February 26, 1855* (Washington, D. C., Printed by B. Tucker, 1855), p4.

26 *Ibid.*, p6.

27 *Ibid.*, p9.

28 Schlereth (ed.), *Material Culture Studies in America*; Ivor Noël Hume, *Guide to Artifacts of Colonial America* (New York: Knopf Publishers, 19).

Chapter 5

1 Bezdek, *American Swords and Sword Makers*, pp15–17, 37–55, 63–227.

2 Gardner, *Five Centuries of Gunsmiths, Swordsmiths, and Armourers, 1400–1900*, pp237–41; Mowbray, *The American Eagle Pommel Sword*, p33.

3 Gardner, *Five Centuries of Gunsmiths, Swordsmiths, and Armourers, 1400–1900*, pp237–41.

4 *Ibid.*, p31.

5 Christian Aries, *Armes Blanches Militaires Française* (Paris: Libraire Pierre-Petitot, 1966), p33.

6 *Ibid.*, p15.

7 Stephen N. Fliegel, *Arms and Armor* (Cleveland, Ohio: The Cleveland Museum of Art, 1998), pp116–18.

8 Evangelista, *Encyclopaedia of the Sword*, pp618-19.

9 Hicks, *Nathan Starr*, p11; Peterson, *The American Sword 1775 – 1945*, 268.

10 Advertisement cited in Hicks, *Nathan Starr*, pp12.

11 Gardner, *Five Centuries of Gunsmiths, Swordsmiths, and Armourers 1400–1900*, p99.

12 Bezdek, *American Swords and Sword Makers*, pp11, 16, 200–03; Peterson, *The American Sword 1775-1945*, p268.

13 Peterson, *The American Sword 1775-1945*, p268; Hicks, *Nathan Starr*, p19.

14 Naval Agent Joseph Hull to Nathan Starr, 18 May 1808. Transcript in the hand of Joseph Hull, National Archives, Washington, D.C.

15 Contract between Nathan Starr and United States Navy, 1813, National Archives, Washington, D.C.

16 Hicks, *Nathan Starr*, p16.

17 Bezdek, *American Swords and Sword Makers*, pp179.

18 *Ibid.*, pp188-9.

19 Peterson, *The American Sword 1775-1945*, p262.

20 1798 Tax Records. National Archives. Washington, D.C.

21 Gardner, *Five Centuries of Gunsmiths, Swordsmiths, and Armourers, 1400–1900*, p99.

22 Peterson, *The American Sword 1775-1945*, p234.

23 *Ibid.*, p236.

24 Contract Proposals 1816. National Archives. Washington, D.C.

25 *Ibid.*

26 *Ibid.*

27 Bezdek, *American Swords and Sword Makers*, pp99, 103; James McHenry to Wm John Harris, 10 August 1797, transcript in the hand of James Henry, National Archives, Washington, D. C.; James Henry to Wm John Harris, 4 May 1797, transcript in the hand of James Henry, National Archives, Washington, D.C.

28 Contract between John Martin and the United States Navy, National Archives, Washington, D.C.

29 James Henry to Wm Robert Gill, 1799, in the hand of James Henry, transcript in the hand of James Henry, National Archives, Washington, D.C.

30 Contract Proposals 1816, National Archives. Washington, D. C.; Peterson, *The American Sword 1775-1945*, p251.

31 Bezdek, *American Swords and Sword Makers*, pp86, 168, 216.

32 J. Rodgers, to Robert Dingie, 26 April 1831, transcript in the hand of J. Rodgers, National Archives, Washington, D.C.

33 *Ibid.*

34 Gilkerson, *Boarders Away with Steel*, p43.

Bibliography

Manuscript Sources

National Archives, Washington, D. C., Record Group 45. Records of the Office of Naval Records and Library.

—————, Record Group 74. Records of the Bureau of Ordnance.

—————, Record Group 92. Naval Ordnances.

Public Record Office, London, Administration 1: Admiralty, and Ministry of Defence,

Navy Department: Correspondence and Papers.

—————, Administration 2: Admiralty Out Letters.

—————, War Office 3: Office of the Commander-in-Chief: Out-letters.

—————, War Office 44: Ordnance Office and War Office: Correspondence.

—————, War Office 46: Ordnance Office: Out-letters.

—————, War Office 47: Ordnance Office: Board of Ordnance: Minutes.

—————, War Office 48 & 53: Accounts of Treasurers.

—— ——, War Office 123: General Orders, 1805–1857.

—————, War Office 185 & 286: Ministry of Supply.

Printed Documents

Bannerman, Francis, *Bannerman Catalog of Military Goods, 1927* (Original manuscript reproduced by DBI Books, Inc., Northfield, Illinois, 1930).

Callo, Joseph F., *Nelson Speaks: Admiral Lord Nelson in his Own Words* (Annapolis, Maryland: Naval Institute Press, 2001).

Diderot, Denis, *A Diderot Pictorial Encyclopedia of Trades and Industry* (Original manuscript reproduced by Dover Publications, Inc., New York, 1959).

Dudley, William S. (ed), *The Naval War of 1812: A Documentary History, Volume 1* (Washington, D.C.: Government Printing Office, 1985).

Esquemeling, John, *Bucaniers of America* (National Archives. Washington, D.C., 1684. Microfilm).

Hutton, Alfred, *The Sword and the Centuries* (London: Grant Richards, 1901).

Jameson, J. Franklin. *Dictionary of United States History, 1492–1899* (Boston, Massachusetts: History Publishing Company, 1899).

Knox, Dudley W. (ed.), *Naval Documents related to the United States Wars with the Barbary Powers:* 5 vols (Washington, D.C.: Government Printing Office, 1941).

Marey, Colonel, *Memoir on Swords* (London: John Weale Publishers, 1860).

Mountaine, W., *The Seaman's Vade-Mecum, and Definitive War by Sea* (London: Mont & Page, 1767).

Oliver, Philip, *Official Records of the Union and Confederate Navies In the War of the Rebellion*, Volumes 1, 2, 4, 5, 7, 8, 13, 15, 18, 19, 21, 23, 24 (Washington D.C.: Government Printing Office, 1894–1922).

O'Rourke, Matthew J., *A New System of Sword Exercise with a Manual of the Sword for Officers* (New York: J. Gray & Company, 1872).

Silver, George, *Paradoxes of Defence* (London, 1599. Original manuscript reproduced by the Shakespeare Association, London, 1933).

Swanson, Claude A. (ed.), *Naval Documents Related to the Quasi-War between the United States and France: Naval Operations from April 1799 to July 1799* (Washington, D.C.: Government Printing Office, 1936).

Tracey, Nicholas, *The Naval Chronicle: The Contemporary Record of the Royal Navy at War*, Volumes 1 – 5 (London: Chatham Publishing, 1998).

United States Congress. *Addresses on the presentation of the sword of General Andrew Jackson to the Congress of the United States, delivered in the Senate and House of representatives, February 26, 1855* (Washington, D.C.: B. Tucker, 1855).

Memoirs

Hoffman, Captain Frederick, *A Sailor of King George: The Journals of Captain Frederick Hoffman RN 1793 – 1814* (London: Chatham Publishing, 1999).

Leech, Samuel. *Thirty Years from Home or a Voice from the Main Deck* (London: H.G. Collins, 1851).

Secondary Sources

Books

Albaugh, William A. III, *Confederate Edged Weapons* (New York: Harper & Brothers, 1960).

—————, *A Photographic Supplement of Confederate Swords* (Orange, Virginia: Moss Publications of Orange, 1979).

Altmayer, Jay P., *American Presentation Swords* (Mobile, Alabama: The Rankin Press, 1958).

Anonymous. Springfield Armory National Historic Site. (Springfield, Massachusetts: Discovery Software Inc., 1998, accessed 3 July 2000); available from http://www.nps.gov/spar/; Internet.

Annis, P.G.W., *Naval Swords: British and American Naval Edged Weapons 1660–1815* (Harrisburg, Pennsylvania: Stackpole Books, 1970).

Archibald, E.H.H., *The Wooden Fighting Ship in the Royal Navy, AD 897–1860* (New York: Arco Publishing Company, 1971).

Aries, Christian, *Armes Blanches Militaires Française* (Paris: Librairie Pierre-Petitot, 1966).

Aylward, J.D., *The Small-Sword in England: its History, its Forms, its Makers, and its Masters* (New York: Hutchinson's Scientific & Technical Publications, 1945).

Belote, Theodore T., *American and European Swords in the Historical Collections of the United States National Museum* (Washington, D.C.: Government Printing Office, 1932).

Bentonrist, James Gilch, *The Fabrication of Small Arms for the United States Service*, prepared under the direction of Stephen V. Benét. Assisted by J. E. Greer, D. A. Lyle and E. S. Allin (New York: Benchmark Publishing Company Inc., 1970).

Bezdek, Richard H., *American Swords and Sword Makers* (Boulder, Colorado: Paladin Press, 1994).

———, *Swords and Sword Makers of the War of 1812* (Boulder, Colorado: Paladin Press, 1997).

Binford, Lewis R., *An Archaeological Perspective* (New York: Seminar Press, 1972).

Blair, Claude, *European & American Arms c. 1100 – 1850* (New York: Crown Publishers, Inc., 1962).

Bosanquet, Captain Henry T.A., *The Naval Officer's Sword* (London: Her Majesty's Stationery Office, 1955).

Bradford, Ernle, *The Story of the Mary Rose* (New York: W.W. Norton and Company, 1982).

———, *Nelson: The Essential Hero* (London: Wordsworth Editions Limited, 1999).

Bridenbaugh, Carl, *The Colonial Craftsman* (New York: New York University Press, 1990).

Brown, John Brewer, *Swords Voted to Officers of the Revolution by the ... Continental Congress, 1775–1784* (Washington, D.C.: The Society of the Cincinnati, 1955).

Brown, Rodney Hilton. *American Polearms, 1526-1865: The Lance, Halberd, Spontoon, Pike, and Naval Boarding Weapons* (New Milford, Connecticut: N. Flayderman & Co. Inc., 1967).

Browning, Dr. Robert M, Jr. 'The Confederate States Navy Department', in Dr William N. Still (ed), *The Confederate Navy, The Ships, Men and Organization, 1861 – 1865* (London: Conway Maritime Press, 1997).

Burton, Richard F., *The Book of the Sword* (New York: Dover Publications, Inc., 1884).

Cain, Emily, *Ghost Ships: Hamilton and Scourge: Historical Treasures From the War of 1812* (New York: MUSSON/Toronto, 1983).

Calvert, Brigadier Michael, *A Dictionary of Battles, 1715–1815* (London: New England Library, 1978).

Canney, Donald L., *Lincoln's Navy: The Ships, Men and Organization, 1861-65* (London: Conway Maritime Press, 1998).

———, *Sailing Warships of the US Navy* (Annapolis, Maryland: Naval Institute Press, 2001).

Case, Paul Foster, *Great Seal of the United States* (Washington, D.C.: Government Printing Office, 1976)

Chandler, David (ed.), *Dictionary of Battles: The World's Key Battles from 405 BC to Today* (New York: Henry Holt and Company, 1987).

Cotter, John L., and J. Paul Hudson, *New Discoveries at Jamestown: Site of the First Successful English Settlement in America* (Washington, D.C.: National Park Service, 1957).

———, *Archaeological Excavations at Jamestown, Colonial National Historical Park and Jamestown National Historic Site* (Washington,

D.C.: National Park Service, 1958).

Cromwell, Giles, *The Virginia Manufactory of Arms* (Charlottesville, Virginia: The University Press of Virginia, 1975).

Davidson, H. R. Ellis, *The Sword in Anglo Saxon England* (Oxford: Oxford University Press. 1962).

Davis, Paul K., *Encyclopedia of Invasions and Conquests from Ancient Times to the Present* (Denver, Colorado: ABC Clio, 1996).

Deetz, James, *In Small Things Forgotten: The Archaeology of Early American Life* (New York: Anchor Books, 1977).

Delgado, James P., *Encyclopedia of Underwater and Maritime Archaeology* (New Haven, Connecticut: Yale University Press, 1997).

Evangelista, Nick, *The Encyclopedia of the Sword* (Westport, Connecticut: Greenwood Press, 1995).

Fliegel, Stephen N., *Arms and Armor* (Cleveland, Ohio: The Cleveland Museum of Art, 1998).

Fuller, Claude E., *Springfield Shoulder Arms 1795 – 1865* (New York: S and S Firearms, 1930).

Gardner, Robert Edward, *Five Centuries of Gunsmiths, Swordsmiths, and Armourers, 1400 –1900* (Columbus, Ohio: Long's College Book Company, 1950).

Gilkerson, William, *Boarders Away with Steel: The Edged Weapons and Polearms of the Classical Age of Fighting Sail, 1626–1826, Tracing their Development in the Navies of England and Northern Europe Through that of the United States* (Lincoln, Rhode Island: Andrew Mowbray, Inc., 1991).

Grafton, Carol Belanger, *Arms & Armour: A Pictorial Archive from Nineteenth Century Sources* (Toronto, Canada: Dover Publications, Inc., 1995).

Hartzler, Daniel D., *Arms Makers of Maryland* (York, Pennsylvania: George Shumway Publisher, 1977).

Haythornthwaite, Philip, and William Younghusband, *Nelson's Navy* (London: Osprey Publishing Ltd., 1993).

Headrick, Daniel R., *The Tools of Empire: Technology and European Imperialism in the Nineteenth Century* (Oxford: Oxford University Press, 1981).

Henretta, James A. and Gregory H. Nobles, *Evolution and Revolution: American Society, 1600 – 1820* (Lexington, Massachusetts: D.C. Heath and Company, 1987).

Hicks, James E., *Nathan Starr, U.S. Sword and Arms Maker* (Mt. Vernon, New York: James E. Hicks Publishing, 1940).

Hickey, Donald R., *The War of 1812: A Short History* (Chicago, Illinois: University of Chicago Press, 1995).

Hickox, Ron G., *Collector's Guide of Ames U.S. Contract Military Edged. Weapons: 1832 –1906* (Brandon, Florida: Ron G. Hickox, 1984).

Hrisoulas, Jim, *The Pattern-Welded Blade: Artistry in Iron* (Boulder, Colorado: Paladin Press, 1994).

Hume, Ivor Noël, *Guide to Artifacts of Colonial America* (New York: Knopf Publishers, 1972).

Ireland, Bernard, *Naval Warfare in the Age of Sail* (London: W.W. Norton & Company, 2000).

Jamestown Rediscovery Project, (Jamestown, Virginia: The Association for the Preservation of Virginia Antiquities, 1997, accessed 3 October 2002); available from http://www.apva.org/ngex/c9halb.html; Internet.

Karcheski, Walter J. Jr, *Arms and Armor in the Art Institute of Chicago* (New York: The Art Institute of Chicago, 1995).

Kauffman, Henry J., *American Axes: A Survey of their Development and their Makers* (Elverson, Pennsylvania: Olde Springfield Shoppe, 1972).

Kohn, George C., *Dictionary of Wars* (New York: University of Oxford Press, 1986).

Lavery, Brian, *The Arming and Fitting of English Ships of War 1600 – 1815* (London: Conway Maritime Press, 1987).

————, *Nelson's Navy: The Ships, Men and Organisation 1793–1815* (London: Conway Maritime Press, 1989).

Lewis, Charles Lee, *The Romantic Decatur* (Oxford: Oxford University Press, 1937).

Lewis, M.A., *A Social History of the Royal Navy, 1793 – 1815* (London, 1960), pp31, 36.

Lloyd, Christopher, *Atlas of Maritime History* (New York: Arco Publishing Company, Inc., 1975).

Lovette, Leland P., *Naval Customs, Traditions and Usage* (Menasha, Wisconsin: George Banta Publishing Company, 1934).

Lyon, David & Rif Winfield, *The Sail & Steam Navy List: All the Ships of the Royal Navy 1815 – 1889* (London: Chatham Publishing, 2004).

Martin, Tyrone G., *A Most Fortunate Ship* (Annapolis, Maryland: Naval Institute Press, 1997).

May, Commander W. E., and P. G. W. Annis, *Swords for Sea Service* (London: Her Majesty's Stationery Office, 1970).

Mayerson, Philip, *Classical Mythology in Literature, Art, and Music* (New York: Scott, Foresman and Company, 1971).

McKee, Christopher, *A Gentlemanly and Honorable Profession: The Creation of the U.S. Naval Officer Corps, 1794-1815* (Annapolis, Maryland: Naval Institute Press, 1991).

Moore, Warren, *Weapons of the American Revolution … and Accoutrements* (New York: Funk & Wangalls, 1967).

Mowbray, E. Andrew, *The American Eagle Pommel Sword* (Lincoln, Rhode Island: Andrew Mowbray, Inc., 1988).

Neumann, George C., *Swords & Blades of the American Revolution* (Harrisburg: Pennsylvania: The Stackpole Company, 1973).

————, and Don Pottinger, *English Weapons & Warfare: 449-1600* (New York: Barnes and Noble, 1966).

Norman, A.V.B., and G.M. Wilson, *Treasures from the Tower of London* (London: Lund Humphries Publishers Ltd., 1982).

Oakshott, Ewart, *The Archaeology of Weapons: Arms & Armor from Prehistory to the Age of Chivalry* (New York: Barnes and Noble, 1960).

————, *A Knight and his Weapons* (Chester Spring, Pennsylvania: Dufour Editions, Inc, 1964).

————, *European Swords* (London: Her Majesty's Stationery Office, 1982).

Palmer, Michael A., *Stoddert's War: Naval Operations During the Quasi-War with France, 1798-1801* (Annapolis, Maryland: Naval Institute Press, 2000).

Parker, Geoffrey, *The Military Revolution: Military Innovations and the Rise of the West, 1500-1800* (Cambridge: Cambridge University Press, 1996).

Peterson, Harold L., *The American Sword 1775 – 1945. A Survey of the Swords Worn by the Uniformed Forces of the United States from the Revolutionary to the Close of World War II* (Philadelphia, Pennsylvania: Ray Riling Arms Books Co., 1954).

————, *Arms and Armour in Colonial America, 1526–1783* (New York: Bramhall House, 1956).

————, *The Book of the Continental Soldier* (Harrisburg: Pennsylvania: The Stackpole Company, 1968).

Rankin, Colonel Robert H., *Small Arms of the Sea Services* (New Milford, Connecticut: N. Flayderman and Co., Inc., 1972).

Reid, William, *Arms and Armor Through the Ages* (New York: Harper and Row Publishers, 1976).

Roberts, Timothy R., *Ancient Civilizations: Great Empires at Their Height* (New York: Smithmark Publishers, 1997).

Roosevelt, Theodore, *The Naval War of 1812* (New York: G.P. Putnam's Sons, 1902).

Schlereth, Thomas J. (ed.), *Material Culture Studies in America* (Walnut Creek, California: Altamira Press, 1996).

Silverstone, Paul H., *The Sailing Navy 1775 –1854* (Annapolis, Maryland: Naval Institute Press, 2001).

Society of the Cincinnati Museum, *Sword and Firearm Collection of the Society of the Cincinnati in the Anderson House Museum, Washington, D.C.* (Washington, D. C.: Society of the Cincinnati, 1965).

Still, Dr. William N., Jr., *The Confederate Navy, The Ships, Men and Organization, 1861-1865* (London: Conway Maritime Press, 1997).

Stone, George Cameron. *A Glossary of the Construction, Decoration and Use of Arms and Armor in all Countries and in all times* (New York: Jack Brussel Publisher, 1935).

Thomson, Charles, 'Remarks and Explanations, of the Great Seal of the United States', reproduced in Paul Foster Case. *Great Seal of the United States* (Washington, D.C.: Government Printing Office, 1976).

Tily, James C., *Uniforms of the United States Navy* (New York: Thomas Yoseloff, 1964).

Troiani, Don, *Don Troiani's Soldiers in America 1754 – 1865* (Harrisburg, Pennsylvania: The Stackpole Company, 1998).

Tunis, Edwin, *Weapons: A Pictorial History* (Baltimore, Maryland: The Johns Hopkins University Press, 1954).

US Navy, *Navy Uniform History* (Washington, D.C.: Naval Media Center, 1995).

Wareham, Tom, *The Star Captains: Frigate Command in the Napoleonic Wars* (Annapolis, Maryland: Naval Institute Press, 2001).

Whisker, James B., *Arms Makers of Pennsylvania* (Selinsgrove, Pennsylvania: Susquehanna University Press, 1990).

Wilkinson-Latham, Robert, *Swords and other Edged Weapons* (New York: Arco Publishing Company, Inc., 1978).

Winton, John, *Hurrah for the Life of a Sailor! Life on the Lower Deck of the Victorian Navy* (London: Michael Joseph Limited, 1977).

Articles

Arnold, Ralph E., ' Early American Eagle Head Swords, Part I', *Arms Gazette* (October 1975), pp10–14.

————,'Early American Eagle Head Swords, Part II', *Arms Gazette* (November 1975), pp10–13.

Bingham, Robert W., 'The Evolution of the American Naval

Cutlass', *Museum Notes of the Buffalo Historical Society*, vol. 2, no. 1 (January–March 1953), pp6–8.

Blair, Claude, 'A Royal Swordsmith and Damascener: Diego de Caias', *MET Journal* vol. III (1970), pp149–98;

Credland, A.G., 'Some Swords of the English Civil War with notes on the Origins of the Basket-Hilt', *The International Journal of the Arms and Armour Society*, vol. 10, no. 6 (December 1982), pp196–205.

Guthman, William H., 'Colonial Swords of New England, Part I: Lion Head Pommels', *Man at Arms* (Sept–Oct 1982), pp36–42.

Harding, Anthony, 'Stone, Bronze, and Iron' in *Swords and Hilt Weapons* (New York: Barnes and Noble Books, 1989), pp8–19.

Hickox, Ron G., 'J.S. Baker Naval Cutlass of 1817', *The Gun Report* (October 1979), pp26–8.

Hildred, Alexandra, 'The Material Culture of the *Mary Rose* (1545) as a Fighting Vessel: The Uses of Wood', in *Artefacts from Wrecks: Dated Assemblages from the Late Middle Ages to the Industrial Revolution* (Oxford: Oxbow Monograph no. 84, 1997), pp51–72.

Hopkins, Alfred F., 'Nathan Starr Cutlass of 1808', *Bulletin of the Society of American Sword Collectors*, vol. 3, no. 5 (October 1948), pp4–5.

LaRocca, Donald J., 'The Renaissance Spirit' in *Swords and Hilt Weapons* (New York: Barnes and Noble, 1989), pp44–57.

Lustyik, Andrew F., 'John Bailey – Swordmaker', *The Gun Report* (February 1980), pp12–20.

Martin, Colin J.M., 'The Cromwellian Shipwreck off Duart Point, Mull', in Mark Redknap (ed.), *Artefacts from Wrecks: Dated Assemblages from the Late Middle Ages to the Industrial Revolution* (Oxford: Oxbow Monograph no. 84, 1997), pp167–80.

Medicus, Philip, 'Lewis Prahl, Early American Armsmaker', *Bulletin of the Society of American Sword Collectors*. vol. 1, no. 2 (March 1947), pp2–3.

Milward, Clement, 'Further Notes on London and Hounslow Swordsmiths', *Apollo*, vol. XXXV, no. 208 (April 1942), pp93–6.

Mont, John S. du., 'J. Bailey: America's Famous Revolutionary War Sword Maker', *Man at Arms* (March/April 1987), pp18–25.

Nelson, Daniel A., '*Hamilton & Scourge*: Ghost Ships of the War of 1812', *National Geographic*, vol. 163, no. 3 (March 1983), pp289–313.

North, Anthony, 'Barbarians and Christians', *Swords and Hilt Weapons* (New York: Barnes and Noble, 1989), pp8–20.

———, 'From Rapier to Smallsword', *Swords and Hilt Weapons* (New York: Barnes and Noble, 1989), pp58–72.

———, 'Seventeenth Century Europe', *Swords and Hilt Weapons* (New York: Barnes and Noble, 1989), pp72–84.

———, 'Eighteenth and Nineteenth Century Europe', *Swords and Hilt Weapons*. (New York: Barnes and Noble, 1989), pp84–96.

Panseri, Carlo, 'Damascus Steel in Legend and in Reality', *Gladius*, vol. IV (1965), pp5–66.

Pell, Stephen H.P., 'American Pole Arms or Shafted Weapons', *Bulletin of the Fort Ticonderoga Museum*, vol. 5 no. 3 (July 1939), pp66–103.

Peterson, Harold L., 'The American Cutlass', *Bulletin of the Society of American Sword Collectors*, vol. 3, no. 2 (October 1949), pp10–15.

Ringer, James, 'Phip's Fleet', *National Geographic*, vol. 198, no. 2 (August 2000), pp72–81.

Spina, James D., 'America's First Swordmaker', *The Gun Report* (March 1975), pp56–8.

Tofts, Wile J., 'The Sword-Blademakers at Hounslow Sword Mill', *The Hounslow Chronicles*, vol. VI, no. 1 (Spring 1983), pp12–14.

Wingwood, Allan J., '*Sea Venture* Second interim report – part 2: the artifacts', *International Journal of Nautical Archaeology and Underwater Exploration*, vol. 15, no. 2 (May 1986), pp149–51.

Theses

Lusardi, Wayne, 'Shipwrecked Swords: An Examination of Edged Weaponry Recovered from Spanish Colonial Vessels and Archaeological Sites, 1492 – 1733.' M.A. thesis, Program in Maritime History and Nautical Archaeology, East Carolina University, Greenville, North Carolina, 1998.

Wolfe, Sarah, 'Historiographical and Cultural Study of Anglo American Naval Edged Weapons, 1797 – 1815.' M.A. thesis. Program in Maritime History and Nautical Archaeology, East Carolina University, Greenville, North Carolina, April 2001.

Index